Cambridge Elements ⹀

Elements in Histories of Emotions and the Senses

edited by
Rob Boddice
Tampere University
Piroska Nagy
Université du Québec à Montréal (UQAM)
Mark Smith
University of South Carolina

BEYOND COMPASSION

Gender and Humanitarian Action

Dolores Martín-Moruno
University of Geneva

Swiss National
Science Foundation

CAMBRIDGE
UNIVERSITY PRESS

Shaftesbury Road, Cambridge CB2 8EA, United Kingdom

One Liberty Plaza, 20th Floor, New York, NY 10006, USA

477 Williamstown Road, Port Melbourne, VIC 3207, Australia

314–321, 3rd Floor, Plot 3, Splendor Forum, Jasola District Centre,
New Delhi – 110025, India

103 Penang Road, #05–06/07, Visioncrest Commercial, Singapore 238467

Cambridge University Press is part of Cambridge University Press & Assessment,
a department of the University of Cambridge.

We share the University's mission to contribute to society through the pursuit of
education, learning and research at the highest international levels of excellence.

www.cambridge.org
Information on this title: www.cambridge.org/9781009462242
DOI: 10.1017/9781009417075

When citing this work, please include a reference to the DOI 10.1017/9781009417075

First published 2023

A catalogue record for this publication is available from the British Library

ISBN 978-1-009-46224-2 Hardback
ISBN 978-1-009-41709-9 Paperback
ISSN 2632-1068 (online)
ISSN 2632-105X (print)

Beyond Compassion

Gender and Humanitarian Action

Elements in Histories of Emotions and the Senses

DOI: 10.1017/9781009417075
First published online: November 2023

Dolores Martín-Moruno
University of Geneva

Author for correspondence: Dolores Martín-Moruno, dolores.martinmoruno @unige.ch

Abstract: This is a call to engage with the histories of emotions and the senses, as well as with the new history of experiences, in order to write a gendered history of humanitarian action. This Element challenges essentialist interpretations according to which women have undertaken humanitarian action because of their allegedly compassionate nature. Instead, it shows how humanitarianism has allowed women to participate in international politics by claiming their rights as citizens, struggling against class inequalities, racial segregation and sexual discrimination in the light of disparate feelings such as resentment, hope, trust, shame and indignation. Ultimately, these case studies are understood to represent historically created moral economies of care: distinctive ways of feeling, performing and knowing humanitarianism which have evolved in relation to shifting emotional values associated with what it means to be human. This Element is also available as Open Access on Cambridge Core.

Keywords: gender, humanitarianism, emotions, experiences, care

ISBNs: 9781009462242 (HB), 9781009417099 (PB), 9781009417075 (OC)
ISSNs: 2632-1068 (online), 2632-105X (print)

Contents

1 Helvetic Emotions

I joined the University of Geneva in early 2011, when this institution offered me a postdoctoral position with the remit of introducing the history of emotions as a line of research at the Institute of History of Medicine and Health; a centre which was formerly affiliated to the Faculty of Medicine. My first – and somewhat naïve – impression was that engaging my new colleagues in the history of emotions would be a relatively simple task. After all, the naturalised Swiss physician, literary critic and historian Jean Starobinski (1920–2019) was internationally recognised for having developed the history of medicine in close relation to the study of emotions at the University of Geneva.[1] More specifically, Starobinski devoted an important part of his career to exploring – what I call in this introductory section – 'Helvetic emotions': an expression that I use in order to explore those distinctive affective traits which have come to embody the Swiss national identity.[2] In naming these emotions in this way, I am not defining them as a natural attribute that is inscribed in Swiss people's DNA, but rather as normative social, cultural and political expectations according to which individuals have learnt to feel and express their attachment to their country. But which emotions have contributed to the formation of a characteristically Swiss emotional community, whose legendary foundations can be traced back to the alliance established by the three founding Cantons – Uri, Schwyz and Unterwalden – in the Rütli (also spelt *Grütli* in French and Italian) mountain meadow in 1291?

Amongst the emotions which Starobinski (1966, 84) identified as a main feature of Helvetic physiognomy, he highlighted nostalgia: a painful form of sadness which became a pathological condition amongst Swiss mercenaries in the seventeenth century. While fighting abroad, these soldiers developed a kind of love-melancholy for their homeland mountain landscapes, above all, when they remembered folk melodies such as the *ranz-des-vaches*: a traditional song sung by herdsmen in order to call their cows in the Alpine pastures. As Starobinski (1966, 88) remarked, the medical treatment of nostalgia became 'the occasion to vindicate the Swiss character' by identifying the cause of this homesickness with the different atmospheric pressure felt by those natives from the Alps who had moved to lower countries and who, therefore, suffered from poor blood circulation.[3] Moved by patriotic rhetoric, the physician Johann Jakob Scheuchzer (1672–1733) had no doubt in pointing out that the only

---

[1] The parents of Starobinski were Polish Jews. Although he was born in Geneva, he only received Swiss nationality in 1948.

[2] I have borrowed this expression from a documentary produced by the Swiss filmmaker Jacqueline Veuve entitled 'Les émotions helvétiques' (1991).

[3] Nostalgia was first diagnosed by the Swiss physician Johannes Hofer (1669–1752). See Dodman (2018).

pharmakon for healing nostalgia was to send 'the sick person back home' or – when this was not possible – to inspire 'him with the hope of returning' while 'quartering him on a hill or a tower', where he could 'breathe lighter air'. As Starobinski (1966, 89) reminds us, Scheuchzer's notion of nostalgia reveals the 'first intimations of the future hotel prospectus' through which the Helvetic Confederation would sell to the world market its image as a spa resort, where people could come to restore their bodies through the healthy virtues provided by the clean air and water of its mountains. Thus, nostalgia appears as a central political emotion in the construction of the Romantic image of Switzerland as a kind of Arcadia: a land where its citizens live authentically by feeling in intimate connection with an imagined Alpine virginal nature, as described by the Genevan philosopher Jean-Jacques Rousseau.

Decades before 'the global bloom in the study of the history of emotions' (Plamper 2015, 60), Starobinski was advancing revolutionary theses, such as those that are currently being discussed concerning the relevance of analysing collective sentiments to shed light on the configuration of 'lived national communities' (Kivimäki et al. 2021). Indeed, Starobinski's timely ideas have recently been highlighted by Fernando Vidal (2020) as one of the major intellectual influences that explains the emergence of the new history of emotions in the early twenty-first century. While I agree with Vidal about Starobinski's leading role in the integration of emotions within the historical enterprise, I am less convinced about the repercussion of his ideas within Swiss academia: a milieu where historians have been particularly hesitant to adhere to the emotional turn which has spread through the international research community (Martín-Moruno 2020a, 149).

On my arrival at the University of Geneva, I noticed that I represented an exotic scholarly minority amongst my fellows who seemed to be particularly reluctant to consider the use of the meta-concept of emotion as a worthy category of historical enquiry due to – what they still consider as – its psychological connotations.[4] One can wonder if the difficulties for the take-off of the history of emotions in Switzerland could be explained by the absence of a homogeneous school of cultural history – such as the French Annales school – which could unify the variety of methodological approaches used by German-, French- and Italian-speaking research groups within this country (Dejung 2011, 162). Despite the vitality of Starobinski's legacy, I have only been able to identify a few Swiss historians (Louis-Courvoisier 2019; Maier and Saxer 2007; Prieto 2018 and 2020) who have acknowledged the benefits of the history

---

[4] This critique should be taken seriously to avoid presentist interpretations of the past. A response is outlined in this Element through the exploration of new approaches such as the history of experiences.

of emotions in order to interpret social, cultural and political change and these were mainly based in the German-speaking part of the country, showing the influence exerted by institutions such as the Centre for the History of Emotions based at the Max Planck Institute for Human Development in Berlin. On the Lake Leman side, emotion research is clearly identified with the Swiss Center for Affective Sciences: an interdisciplinary institute hosted by the University of Geneva which gathers together psychologists, neuroscientists, philosophers, political scientists, linguistics, physicians and literary scholars, but which lacks a clear focus on history. My first impression was that the very existence of the history of emotions – as a program whose goal was to demonstrate that feelings are not a universal constant across ages and cultures – was regarded by these specialists as a central attack on their own research. However, I went on to meet some colleagues – and in particular the literary scholar Patrizia Lombardo (1950–2019) – who allowed me to collaborate with this centre and discover that its members were more receptive to emotion history than I had initially thought.

More than twelve years after my *coming out* as a historian of emotions at the University of Geneva, I cannot state that my work has radically transformed the agenda of Swiss historians, who still feel more comfortable with the history of sensibilities developed by Lucien Febvre and his followers.[5] However, I am quite satisfied with the fact that I have created my own team and shared my passion for the history of emotions with my collaborators. I wish to thank them for having embarked on the project which I have led over the last six years; a period that has gone hand in hand with the naturalisation process through which I have become a Swiss citizen. Critically looking to discover the Swissness of my Spanish-made heart, I did not hesitate to follow in Starobinski's steps in order to write a new chapter in the history of Helvetic emotions: those emotions which I consider to have forged an idealised picture of Switzerland as a *Sonderfall* (which literally means 'an exceptional case') amongst its neighbouring European countries because of its geographical, cultural, linguistic, religious and political particularities.

Besides nostalgia, I also remarked that compassion has played a decisive role in the historical configuration of the Helvetic Confederation as a rare non-belligerent country, which has been marked by a strong humanitarian tradition. This aspect of Switzerland particularly caught my attention, as my research

---

[5] Although Febvre (1973) made a plea for the study of the affective life of the past, the new history of emotions has broken its initial affiliation with the history of sensibilities because of the latter's emphasis on intellectual over emotional phenomena. Critical arguments against Febvre's thesis have been advanced by medievalists including Piroska Naggy et al. (1994) and Barbara Rosenwein (2002). To understand the history of emotions as a history of practices rather than a development of Febvre's intellectual history, see Martín-Moruno and Pichel (2019, 4).

focused on understanding the complex relationships established between the histories of modern warfare, gender and medical humanitarianism by considering their evolution in the light of the changing experience of others' pain. Several scholars have already pointed out that the humanitarian impulse emerged as an eighteenth-century culture of compassion when a variety of social activists converted 'the alleviation of human suffering' into 'a defining element of modern society' by advocating for such disparate causes as prison reform, the elimination of 'judicial torture and capital punishment', as well as the abolition of slavery and prostitution (Abruzzo 2011, 1; Barnett 2011, 49; Salvatici 2019, 22). In contrast with other affective experiences related to the pain of others, compassion has been celebrated as the humanitarian feeling par excellence, because it involves an active response to alleviating others' suffering which has been loosely identified with the action of taking care of somebody who is in need. Although Western humanitarianism has stressed since its very beginnings 'its international dimensions as a form of universalism' (Taithe 2006, 80), compassion has mythically portrayed Switzerland as a land inhabited by a handful of do-gooders, who have developed – what they still see as – a peculiar form of feeling politics by being actively concerned with aiding populations who are in a situation of vulnerability. To understand the reasons that lie behind the Swiss appropriation of humanitarian compassion, one should be ready to explore the affective politics of this country from a transnational perspective which connects local concerns with the changing geopolitical order.

Patricia Purtschert and Harald Fischer-Tiné (2015, 4) have already shown to what extent the humanitarian ethos was instrumentalised by Swiss political representatives from the nineteenth century onwards to 'cover up and legitimise its economically oriented politics'. As I argue here, a history of emotions perspective could reinvigorate these arguments by considering the Helvetic compassionate character as a central part of a broader affective repertoire inspired by a 'sentimental Imperialism' (Stoler 2004, 6) which exerted its power by strengthening tender ties with Western colonies which – although they were not officially their own – became a fertile territory for implementing Swiss humanitarian missions. Despite the noble aspirations of humanitarianism, we should not forget that compassion – as well as fellow-feelings such as sympathy – has been essential for maintaining colonial affective bonds throughout the Imperial period, as well as for the negotiation of colonial legacies from the Cold War to the present-day (Martín-Moruno 2022, 8). Inscribed in the idyllic vision of the pristine Swiss Alps as a metaphorical site for cultivating altruistic emotions, compassion has been strategically mobilised by the Helvetic Confederation to shape its national identity as a state that has managed 'to stay aloof from regional and global conflicts in the name of neutrality' (Putschert and Fisher-Tiné 2015, 4).

The adoption of – what Ilaria Scaglia (2020a, 9 and 72) has labelled as – 'an alpine, tempered emotional style' has fashioned the cultural perception of Swiss people as peaceful agents, who have developed specific skills for communicating across linguistic and cultural borders and, consequently, for deliberating 'wisely on weighty issues'.[6] Symbolising healthy moral values that enhance mutual cooperation, the Swiss Alps have not only been rhetorically presented as the natural place to treat the suffering resulting from a myriad of diseases – ranging from nostalgia to tuberculosis – but also 'to improve the physiology of the international system' through 'a peace-building emotional approach' destined to resolve conflicts amongst warring political parties (Scaglia 2020a, 12). Prescribed by a plethora of Swiss-based international organisations and aid agencies as the best remedy for palliating the effects of warfare, compassion has gradually been inscribed as a central marker of the Helvetic Confederation's national habitus. However, the allegedly natural Swiss disposition to alleviate others' pain is not as disinterested as it may initially seem as it has responded to both the internal and external challenges that this country has faced since its constitution as a direct democracy in 1848.

Within Swiss domestic politics, compassion has contributed to the invention of the Swiss humanitarian tradition with the aim of reinforcing cohesion amongst a population which shared neither a common language, nor the same cultural or religious traditions. This became particularly urgent with the outbreak of the First World War (1914–1918), when German and French speaking cantons revealed rivalrous sympathies for the German Empire and the Third French Republic respectively. Despite the neutral status of this country, this ideological division – also known as *Röstigraben* (which refers to the cultural trench marked by the taste for the hashed potatoes that are traditionally made in the German-speaking part of the country) – polarized the Swiss population during the Great War (Cotter 2016, 131). Within this strained political context – which was also aggravated by an economic crisis – humanitarianism provided a sense of national belonging through the enhancement of the principle of neutrality that had been originally adopted by the Swiss cantons during the Congress of Vienna in 1815. Thus, compassion became a sort of social glue which assembled a fragmented population through the idea that this country should fight its own battle in the name of the victims of warfare.

---

[6] This Alpine emotional style can be seen to be the opposite of that described by William Reddy (2001) to explain the rise of an excessive sentimentalism during the French Revolution, which went on to lead to the Regime of Terror.

Compassion has also historically played a pivotal ideological role in Switzerland's international politics by positioning this small Central European country as a 'Samaritan's land of love for refugees' (Fisher-Tiné 2015, 223). The celebration of the Helvetic Confederation as a friendly state, which has traditionally opened its frontiers to welcome refugees, takes its roots in epic episodes such as the internment of the French army of Bourbaki on Swiss territory at the end of the Franco-Prussian War (1870–1871), thanks to the efforts made by the Swiss army in collaboration with the Swiss Red Cross (hereafter SRC). After the orchestration of this first humanitarian relief operation, the rhetorical strategy of Swiss diplomacy was to use compassionate discourse to prevent the invasion of its lands during the First World War, as had occurred in other neutral countries such as Belgium during the German occupation (Leyder 2020, 84). Furthermore, this oriented politics of compassion allowed the reactivation of the Helvetic Confederation's economy through the exploitation of the commercial benefits offered by humanitarian missions such as the internment of seriously injured war prisoners on its territory during the Great War.

However, the multiplication of Swiss humanitarian initiatives throughout this armed conflict contrasted with the increasing fear of immigrants which was popularised through the German notion of *Überfremdung*: a term which is still frequently used by Swiss right-wing political representatives to denounce an imagined foreign infiltration. While the expansion of Swiss humanitarianism during the Great War was justified by the need to provide assistance to war victims – such as refugees – who were 'out of place', paradoxically Swiss immigration politics became more restrictive in order to define this country as a 'transit point' rather than a 'permanent heaven' for people who were on the move (Gatrell 2014; Huber 2018). This shift in Swiss migration policies can be interpreted as a collateral effect of compassion, an emotion whose darkest side has led to the mobilisation of groups of people fuelled by a deep feeling of resentment against a common enemy. Thus, compassionate feelings united those Swiss natives who accused refugees of stealing their jobs and, even, their food during the Great War.

Despite the rise of xenophobia – a form of hate that was particularly cultivated amongst the Swiss elite – the First World War would radically change the emotional geography of the Helvetic Confederation by fashioning the city of Geneva as a site for international reconciliation after the establishment of institutions such as the League of Nations in 1920. This was the first intergovernmental organisation which was founded to avoid the outbreak of future escalations of violence within the global order. Nonetheless, this was not the first time that Geneva hosted an agency that federated international efforts to either prevent or mitigate the consequences of warfare by fostering amicable and sympathetic interactions between worldwide representatives (Scaglia 2020b). A turning point in the history of Swiss compassion was epitomised by the creation of – what we call today – the International Committee of the Red Cross (hereafter ICRC): an institution widely known for having regulated the laws through which civilised warfare should be fought. The establishment of the ICRC headquarters in Geneva definitively turned Switzerland into the cradle of the humanitarian movement through the institutionalisation of compassion as a relief action which should be managed and calculated by charitable agencies, in its own likeness. The adoption of a Swiss flag as the Red Cross emblem – with the red and white colours inverted – to symbolise 'the neutral status of the medical staff and their patients', reveals to what extent compassion had come to crystallise the humanitarian spirit of this country (Gill 2013, 2).

1.1 The Faces of Humanitarian Compassion

Originally, as shown in this poster (see Figure 1), the so-called committee of five was at the head of the ICRC. This was comprised of the founding members of this humanitarian initiative; the army general officer Guillaume-Henri Dufour (1787–1875), the lawyer Gustave Moynier (1826–1910), the military surgeon Louis Appia (1818–1898), the physician Theodore Maunoir (1806–1869) and the philanthropic businessman Henry Dunant (1828–1910) – from right to left. On the upper right-hand side of this visual composition, we can see the image of Dufour who is solemnly represented as the spiritual father of this humanitarian project, even though he was not its original instigator. His omnipresence in this picture can be explained by his influential role in the peaceful resolution of the Swiss Civil War – which has been mythically reproduced in Swiss historiography as 'a bloodless fratricidal conflict' so as to preserve the non-violent image of this country (Prieto 2021, 112). Also known as the Sonderbund War, it confronted the conservative Catholic cantons against liberal ones in November 1847. Its brief duration is usually explained by Dufour's thoughtful military strategy – he was chief of the federal army at that time – which resolved this campaign in only a few weeks. As a sign of his humanity towards those brothers who had dramatically turned into enemies, Dufour (quoted in Leuthy 1848, 314) called for compassion amongst his troops in order to care for the wounded.

Although Dufour believed that the pain of warfare was inherent to the existence of humankind, he was deeply convinced that its awful consequences could be minimised by carefully thinking about the laws that should regulate future armed conflicts. Dufour's ideas show that Western political representatives had started to break with 'the heroic vision of the battlefield in which

physical violence had been traditionally highlighted as noble and glorious'
(Martín-Moruno 2020b, 448). Another exponent of this moral reform of warfare
was the North-American President Abraham Lincoln, who adopted the Lieber
code during the American Civil War (1861–1865) in order to set out rules
amongst Union soldiers. By reasoning in these terms, Dufour – like many of
his contemporaries – was announcing a major shift in the history of pain, as the
infliction of unnecessary suffering in the context of warfare came to be considered as a moral outrage that provoked a violent feeling of disgust amongst
those people who considered themselves to have achieved a higher degree of
civilisation, and, therefore, humanity.[7]

Dufour's dream of humanising the cruelty in which the military universe had
been traditionally rooted would be materialised some years later in a project
sketched out by Henry Dunant in a book entitled *A Memory of Solferino* (1862).
Dunant – who is portrayed on the left-hand side of this poster (see Figure 1) –
wrote this moving account to mobilise public opinion concerning the necessity
of creating an international organisation which could ensure relief assistance to
wounded and sick soldiers regardless of their political orientation, as well as
their legal protection and that of the healthcare agents who provided aid in the
battlefield. Dunant came up with this idea when he found himself in the middle
of the fierce battle of Solferino, which confronted the French Empire and
Piedmont-Sardinian troops against those of the Austro-Hungarian Empire during the Second Italian War of Independence (1859). Although he had initially
travelled to Lombardy to convince Napoleon III to support his failing commercial project in the French colony of Algeria, he suddenly changed his plans
when he witnessed the nightmarish vision of thousands of soldiers agonising on
the battlefield. As they were completely abandoned to their fate, Dunant decided
to coordinate the efforts of the local population – as well as those of other war
tourists like him – to provide these soldiers with some improvised first aid.

As he described in *A Memory of Solferino,* the spectacle of suffering symbolised by this relentless campaign of violence led him to experience the spiritual
revelation which would be at the origins of the creation of the Red Cross
movement: what was urgently needed on the battlefield were corps of healthcare
workers who could facilitate emergency relief assistance. As he was deeply
influenced by the Protestant awakening movement, compassion appeared to
Dunant to be a central emotion linked to the spiritual drama of salvation. Indeed,
in his book, Dunant actualised the parable of the Good Samaritan as an active
commitment to philanthropic work, such as an orchestrated healthcare

---

[7] This shift in the history of pain did not just take place in the military universe, it also occurred in
the experimental domain where scientists led research on animals in the name of humanity
(Boddice 2021, 2; Martín-Moruno 2016a; Moscoso 2012, 56).

A BUNCH OF DREAMERS?

No, five good men and true. The five men who under the leadership of Henry Dunant, started the International Red Cross. In 1859 Henry Dunant, a young Swiss businessman observed the horrors of the battle of Solferino. From these observations he conceived the idea of "relief societies for the purpose of having care given to the wounded in wartime by zealous, devoted and thoroughly qualified volunteers?' Back in Switzerland he convened a committee of five which drew up a list of principles on which to base these relief societies:- humanity, impartiality, neutrality, independence, voluntary service, unity and universality, and decided on a symbol, a red cross on a white background. Today there are 130 Red Cross and, in Muslim countries, Red Crescent, Societies throughout the world. All are founded on the same basic principles. And all are dedicated to achieving a world of peace. The memory of the battle of Solferino still persists however. So the red cross symbolises the protection given in times of war, under the Geneva Conventions. The Conventions basically define the right of both military and civilian personnel in times of war, and stress the impartiality of the help given by Red Cross workers. Medical assistance, relief supplies, help to refugees, tracing and reunification of separated families, and many other forms of aid are given by Red Cross throughout the world.

PRODUCED BY THE NEW ZEALAND RED CROSS SOCIETY WITH ASSISTANCE FROM THE L.J. ARKINSTALL ESTATE

Figure 1 'A Bunch of Dreamers?' (1950–1960), ICRC repository.

response, which could transform the pain of warfare into a positive action. The successful reception of *A Memory of Solferino* was the result of Dunant's ability to turn this literary representation into an advocacy strategy, which had the emotional power to engender compassion as 'a kind of moral imperative' in the reader and make them feel, in this way, compelled 'to undertake ameliorative action' (Laqueur 1989, 176). In other words, Dunant's book became a bestseller because of the performative effects of compassion: an emotion which has precipitated historical change by bringing people together around distant humanitarian causes (Martín-Moruno and Pichel 2019, 195).

This is exactly what occurred when Dufour read *A Memory of Solferino*. He decided to convince his colleagues at the Genevan Society of Public Utility – Appia, Maunoir and Moynier – to join forces with Dunant. Just a year after the publication of *A Memory of Solferino*, they organised a first international conference to discuss with other European representatives the adoption of – what would be called – the first Geneva convention for the amelioration of the condition of the wounded in armies in the field. The initial fourteen signatories of this document – Switzerland, Baden, Belgium, Denmark, Spain, France, Hesse, Italy, Netherlands, Portugal, Prussia and Württemberg, as well as the United Kingdom and Sweden, which joined a few months later – also accepted the challenge of creating their own national Red Cross societies to palliate the shortcomings of their military medical services in the case of warfare.

As portrayed in this poster (see Figure 1), the silhouette of Dufour – who was unanimously elected as the first President of the ICRC – as well as those of Moynier, Appia, Dunant and Maunoir, is visually associated with the dream that compassion could triumph over the pain represented by warfare and, therefore, with the emergence of humanitarian sensibility as a movement which has historically appeared to be in intimately related to a moral belief in a shared humanity. Linked with the moral progress of mankind through the Enlightenment concept of civilisation, compassion became the affective criterion used by these ICRC members to measure our humanness: our desire to help others. However, we must remain cautious about the concept of 'civilisation' because – as Starobinski remarked (1993, 18) – it disguises the barbarism it masks: 'this means that the (. . .) defense of civilisation can in certain circumstances justify the recourse to violence', because 'all that resists or threatens civilisation, is monstrous, absolute evil'. Despite the notion of civilisation being presented at its origins as 'a secularised substitute for religion' (Rodogno 2020, 73), it remained deeply anchored in the conception of compassion which was theorised by the theologian Tertullian at the end of the second century to refer to the suffering that Christians shared with Jesus Christ and which, thus, went on to form an emotional community (Barnes and Falconer 2020, 93). The Latin term *compassio* was coined to denote the misericordia felt specifically by humans towards others who resembled them (Konstant 2001, 106). In its original sense, compassion reveals its exclusive nature particularly well, as Christians – like Tertullian – could only feel this emotion for wrongly injured persons who also professed the same religion as them. Compassion was not an emotion that they could feel for pagans as they remained their enemies and, therefore, did not deserve any commiseration.

Dufour, Dunant, Maunoir, Appia and Moynier insisted on stressing the universality of the values supported by the Red Cross movement from its inception, in order to reinforce Swiss neutrality. However, this visual composition reminds us that their use of the concept of civilisation – as well as related notions such as humanity, humanitarianism and, even, compassion – cannot be critically contextualised as an apolitical concept. As Rob Boddice (2021, 1) has pointed out, the shifting meaning of what it means to be and feel like a human has always implied decisions made by groups of persons who claim to be specialists because they are able to discern humans from those who are excluded from belonging to humanity. This is particularly well represented in Figure 1, an image that depicts the necessity of looking like the founding members of the Red Cross movement to become a spokesperson for humanitarianism – and, therefore, an expert on the values, such as compassion, that embody the whole of humanity. Despite their contribution to establishing the laws of warfare, this poster's representation of the ICRC's founding members appears to be extremely problematic in our present-day society because it associates humanitarian compassion with five white men from Geneva's bourgeoisie, who were all strongly influenced by Protestant religious ideals and their colonial ambitions. From my partial perspective – as a twenty-first century Feminist – the image projected by this poster irremediably drives me to ask you the question which is at the core of the next section and which was also the departure point for my own research into the history of humanitarian aid.

1.2 Where Are the Women in the Humanitarian Movement?

Rephrasing the query that Feminist scholars – such as Cynthia Enloe (1989) – have formulated in International Relations, one can only wonder what place women occupy within the humanitarian movement, as decision-making appears to have been an exclusively male privilege. Dunant provides us with some clues for solving this mystery in *A Memory of Solferino* when he describes the voluntary action undertaken by the women of Castiglione to assist those who were wounded in this battle:

> It must not be thought that the lovely girls and kind women of Castiglione, devoted as they were, saved from death many of the wounded and disfigured, but still curable, soldiers to whom they gave their help. All they could do was to bring a little relief to a few of them. What was needed there was not only weak and ignorant women, but, with them and beside them, kindly and

experienced men, capable, firm, already organised, and in sufficient numbers
to get to work at once in an orderly fashion. In that case many of the
complications and fevers which so terribly aggravated wounds originally
slight, but very soon mortal, might have been avoided (Dunant 1947, 121)

What Dunant is telling us about the benevolent girls and women of Castiglione
is that – despite their great Christian devotion – their care for these wounded
soldiers was completely ineffective and actually inflicted further harm instead
of doing anything to alleviate their suffering. What was needed – insisted
Dunant – were skilled men who could supervise their work and take firm
decisions in their name. Although Dunant's words were surely not egregious
amongst late–nineteenth century Western audiences, the expansion of gender
studies from the 1980s onwards enables us to analyse them as the result of the
patriarchal system: literarily 'meaning the rule of the father', but which 'also
extends the authority of men to exercise power and dominate women through
control of society's governmental, social, economic, religious and cultural
institutions' (Cohn 2012, 4). This is a system of power relations which has
reduced women to playing a subaltern role, because they have been subjected to
the hegemony of another more powerful class, which – in this case – is
represented by men like Dunant who have traditionally shaped humanitarian
organisations as a male territory.

Besides Dunant's words, the impact of the patriarchal system within the Red
Cross movement is particularly manifest at the ICRC archives. When I started
my project, I felt really frustrated after several exchanges with the ICRC
archivist who told me that official records rarely preserved information about
female participation in emergency relief operations. This lack of archival
sources reveals that women were not only consciously removed from the
ICRC's collective memory, but also – and most significantly – from positions
of responsibility. There have only been a few ICRC female delegates and the
first one, Jeanne Egger (1925–), was appointed to this position in 1963: around
one hundred years after the creation of this institution. Even if women have
played a secondary role within the ICRC, there are a few exceptions, such as
Marguerite Frick-Cramer (1887–1963), Pauline Chapponière-Chaix (1850–
1934), Suzanne Ferrière (1886–1970) and Lucie Odier (1886–1984) who joined
its board because of their patrician family backgrounds. This reveals to what
extent social class – alongside gender – has played a pivotal role as a criterion in
the selection of this agency's representatives. Although women have actively
participated in the field of operations, the vast majority of their stories have
remained in the shadows and have, therefore, fallen into oblivion.

Despite my initial frustration, I wish to express my gratitude to the ICRC
archivist who warned me that women had been excluded from the records,

because rectifying these silences which have shaped humanitarian history went on to become my main motivation for carrying out my research project. Although official reports were rarely written by women and only sporadically mention them, other sources allow us to retrace their actions: journals, letters, autobiographies, drawings, photographic albums, films, graphic novels, oral records, as well as personal belongings. These sources, which I have gathered together with the members of my team, have provided us with a unique opportunity to create – what I call, rephrasing the title of Virginia Woolf's seminal essay – an archive of one's own. This Feminist-oriented archive constitutes the material foundations of this Element and organises its sections around different cultures of humanitarian aid, in which care has historically evolved in relation to shifting ideals about who deserves to be considered as a member of humanity. Methodologically, this archive of our own has given us room to analyse sources situated halfway between the private and the public sphere and, thus, made it possible to get closer to the universe of emotions, sensations, perceptions, memories and thoughts of a colourful palette of female activists.

A detailed analysis of this corpus of sources reveals that – despite its Helvetic reverberations – compassion was neither just the exclusive preserve of the Red Cross movement, nor that of a bunch of Genevan men such as the ICRC's founding members. In so saying, I am not considering compassion as merely a concept 'which exists only beyond the point at which it attains a linguistic status' – as defended by Starobinski (1966, 81) – but, above all, as a practice 'emerging from bodily dispositions conditioned by a social context, which always have cultural and historical specificity' (Frevert 2016, 56; Scheer 2012, 193). By regarding compassion as a practice – which has been performed by both individuals and groups – one of my main objectives has been to contribute to the practice turn announced within humanitarian history. Thinking humanitarianism from below opens, thus, the door to contextualising how humanitarian agents actually operated in contexts of emergency, shedding light on their 'ethical dilemmas' when they worked 'with governments and opposition groups', as well as considering 'how true' they remained to 'their declared humanitarian principles' (Taithe and Borton 2015, 217).

Furthermore, looking at emotions – such as compassion – as humanitarian practices appears to give us a great opportunity to carefully examine, from a gender approach, the distribution of responsibilities within relief operations according to a sexual division of labour. This division has been justified by 'the sacrosanct law of sexual difference' that has 'preserved the model of true femininity which was at the heart of the bourgeois family' (Martín-Moruno 2023a). Beyond the private realm, this ideology has also served to establish separate spheres of activity for women and men within the long history of humanitarianism by appealing to their allegedly distinct biological destinies. Although 'the passion for compassion' (Arendt 2006a, 222; Barnett 2011, 50) has been claimed as the driving force that lies behind the humanitarian action performed by both female and male relief agents, the second section of this Element explores how women have specifically translated this emotion into a set of caring practices, which were conceived as an extension of their duties in the private sphere where they had traditionally been in charge of looking after the members of their family (Martín-Moruno et al. 2020, 6). By taking the healthcare reform led by British nurse Florence Nightingale (1820–1910) at the Scutari Hospital during the Crimean War (1853–1856) as a departure point, Section 2 examines the making of the foundational model according to which female relief agents have learned to think, feel and act within the humanitarian movement. Although Nightingale demonstrated exceptional scientific competences and initially felt contempt for the project launched by the ICRC's founding members, Dunant did not hesitate to praise her maternal virtues to assimilate them into the archetype of femininity which he wanted to cultivate within this movement. As Section 2 shows, Nightingale's model went on to be inherited by future generations of female humanitarians who also learned how to feel like compassionate mothers destined to provide care to the victims of warfare mainly – but not exclusively – because of its worldwide promotion by the Red Cross. However, the identification of femininity with compassion has ended up reproducing gender stereotypes and disguising women humanitarians' motivations for aiding distant others, which included: claiming their rights – whether as professional workers or citizens – struggling against class inequalities, racial segregation and sexual discrimination.

Section 3 moves the focus from compassion towards experience to embrace a polyphonic history of humanitarian action which explores the need to help distant strangers through the conflictual memories of the Afro-American nurse Salaria Kea (1913–1991) and the Swiss volunteer Elisabeth Eidenbenz (1913–2011). By navigating through the 'long Second World War' (Humbert et al. 2021),[8] Kea's and Eidenbenz's missions allow us to explore the transnational circulation of humanitarian experiences through non-Western conflicts such as the Second Italo-Ethiopian war (1935–1936), internal wars such as the Spanish Civil War (1936–1939) and – what we traditionally refer to as – the Second World War (1939–1945), as well as their painful negotiation by present-day audiences. These two case studies enable us to discover models of female humanitarian action which were 'anchored in local and vernacular forms arising

---

[8] This periodisation aims to identify transfers of humanitarian practices and experiences from the Japanese invasion of Manchuria (1931–1932) through to the Korean War (1950–1953).

from charity work combined with often more political forms of solidarity' (Taithe 2019, 1782). Oriented by a human-rights approach, Kea and Eidenbenz advocated for an ideal of humanity which was fuelled by hope for a future world where justice would repair the harm that Totalitarianism had caused to victims of atrocities during the long Second World War. Thus, Kea's and Eidenbenz's actions challenge 'persistent myths' according to which humanitarianism has to be conceived as neutral to be labelled as truly humanitarian (Slim 2020).

Section 4 invites us to discover other cultures of humanitarianism, such as that represented by *Médecins sans Frontières* [Doctors without Borders] (hereafter MSF). This organisation reshaped humanitarianism within a new vision of humanity, which embraced the suffering of – what used to be called – the Third World, by negotiating the traumatic legacies of Western Imperialism during the decolonisation process through emotions such as guilt and shame. Although the initial members of this organisation actively participated in the events of May 1968 in Paris and, therefore, could have been expected to be more sensitive to gender issues, this section shows that, until very recently, MSF has remained associated with a group of male adventurers. To shed light on the reasons lying behind female underrepresentation and the lack of female visibility, this section examines the case studies of the French surgeon Christiane Marot (1941–?), a female volunteer who joined the ICRC mission in Biafra which was at the origins of this organisation, and the French dental surgeon Juliette Fournot (1954–), who was head of the MSF medical mission in Afghanistan during the Soviet invasion. Eclipsed by mediatic figures such as Bernard Kouchner (1939–), the few references to Marot that I have been able to identify are still plagued by gender stereotypes which stress her tender and feminine nature, rather than her competences. Even though Fournot's medical operation has received more attention, she had to work in a masculine milieu by playing with gender expectations about what a woman humanitarian should look like to inspire trust amongst local populations.

Section 5 lets us jump from the end of the Cold War to the ongoing Mediterranean crisis to examine contemporary citizen-aid groups which have rescued people on the move in the Mediterranean, such as that led by the German captain Pia Klemp (1983–) aboard the vessel known as the *Iuventa*. Embracing a revolutionary culture of care, Klemp introduces herself as an outraged activist who is one part of an anti-fascist fight against the racist politics governing the Mediterranean: the place where the European Union (hereafter EU) has declared real warfare against people who are frequently referred to as irregular migrants. Although Klemp's role as captain could give the impression that we have achieved gender equality in the twenty-first century, this section shows to what extent her presence in the Mediterranean perturbs EU representatives. Openly declaring herself to be a feminist and a vegan, Klemp's rescue missions give us the opportunity to examine a posthumanist form of care. By anchoring her activism in values such as solidarity, Klemp denounces the necropolitics fostered by EU powers against those beings which are regarded as non-human – whether if they are migrants or animals – to justify their sacrifice in the name of the neoliberal order.

The case studies which I have selected for this Element are not aimed at providing an exhaustive historical vision of female participation in relief operations. Instead, they have been selected to epistemologically approach different cultures of humanitarian aid that represent different and, even, competing 'moral economies of care': distinctive 'modes of thinking, feeling, and acting' (Boddice 2016, 13) within the humanitarian movement which have historically evolved in relation to shifting ideals about humanity. Despite care being widely associated with nursing, my conception is inspired by Berenice Fisher and Joan C. Tronto's (1990, 40) broader definition: 'a species activity that includes everything that we do to maintain, continue, and repair our "world" so that we can live in it as well as possible'. This category of care is flexible enough to embrace a 'world' which 'includes our bodies, ourselves, and our environment'. Thus, care appears to be a useful category not only for historically contextualising women humanitarians' experiences – including their emotional dimensions – from a gender approach, but also for interpreting these experiences as a valuable knowledge gained by practice which has been guided by and, thus, has evolved in the light of diverse moral economies. Either aimed at removing or relieving the pain of different collectives – soldiers, refugees, 'third world' populations, migrants and, even, our blue planet – these moral economies of care have historically incarnated the shifting moral sense of what it has meant to feel like a human within the humanitarian movement.

Although the studies gathered together in this Element deal with the contribution of women to humanitarian history, my objective is not to associate care with a female disposition, but rather to rectify women humanitarians' lack of visibility and deconstruct the gender stereotypes according to which they have been frequently represented. What we can learn from these stories is that the intersection between gender and the histories of emotions and the senses, as well as the new history of experiences, provides us with a privileged perspective from which to disrupt the traditional meaning of 'civilisation in the image of the male, white, well-off, educated human' and, thus, grant women with 'the status of being fully human' actors within the history of humanitarian aid (Bourke 2015, 16 and 18).

2 Gendering Humanitarian Compassion

In *Gendering Global Humanitarianism*, the editors (Möller et al. 2020, 298) complain that 'mainstream histories of humanitarianism (. . .) have failed to engage with the notions, practices and meanings of compassion that numerous women' have mobilised through their engagement 'in philanthropy, voluntarism and care work' since the nineteenth century. As Abigail Green (2014, 1162) has remarked, the absence of any reflection on compassion can be explained by the fact that most of the scholars who have explored the emergence of humanitarian sensibility have not supported their assumptions with research conducted in the history of emotions. In spite of this, several works do contextualise the gendered, religious and national dimensions of compassion to shed light on the specific motivations that women have had to help fellow humans. For instance, Annemieke van Drenth and Francisca de Haan (1999) have shown how compassion allowed early female philanthropists – such as Elisabeth Fry (1780–1845) and Josephine Butler (1828–1906) – to develop a 'caring power' by engaging in prison reform and the abolitionist movement against prostitution, respectively. Closely linked to Michel Foucault's notion of pastoral power, this caring power has enabled Christian and upper-class women to participate in social reform by advocating an essentialist vision of femininity in which compassion appears inscribed as a natural marker of female gender identity. On her side, Rebecca Gill (2013, 20) has noticed how the 'association between female compassion, women's suffrage and the delivery of overseas aid' became 'a salient feature' in the initial stages of the British Red Cross. As Ute Frevert (2011, 100) reminds us, the cultural association of tender feelings with the female sex – which operated in modern societies – gave women an opportunity to expand their caring activities beyond the private sphere; namely, into the realm of nursing and social work. Thus, Frevert's 'emotional topographies of gender' provide us with a useful theoretical framework for understanding how naturalising discourses and representations of female compassion were intended to justify women's participation in relief operations (Frevert 2011, 105).

By regarding compassion as a discursive practice which has infused 'new narrative forms aimed at mediating compassion and love' in the nineteenth century (Taithe 2006, 86), this section starts by analysing Dunant's *A Memory of Solferino* and Nightingale's *Letters from the Crimea* – as well as other writings by Nightingale – from a gender approach. Putting Dunant's book into dialogue with Nightingale's war accounts, my objective is to retrace the invention of the foundational model of female relief action through the performative effects of compassion and – more specifically – its formulation through the Christian virtue of mercy. Even though international agencies have presented compassion as 'a constant devoid of history' (Taithe 2006, 79), an intersectional approach can allow us to comprehend how this emotion has been reshaped in relation to the gender, class, national, racial and religious interests that were represented by a variety of female relief agents in the context of the Crimean War, the Franco-Prussian War and the First World War.

2.1 Who Cares about Soldiers' Suffering?

Although, in *A Memory of Solferino*, Dunant refers to the women of Castiglione as ignorant and weak, he praises the virtues of leading female figures who were also concerned about the inhuman treatment provided to injured and ill soldiers during warfare. In particular, he mentions the Grand Duchess Elena Pavlovna of Russia (1784–1803) and the British nurse Florence Nightingale. Both of them organised corps of female volunteers during the Crimean War: a conflict which confronted the Russian Empire and the Kingdom of Greece against the alliance formed by the Ottoman Empire with Piedmont-Sardinia, the French and the British Empires. While Pavlovna made a call for women to join the Order of the Exaltation of the Cross in order to serve in Russian military hospitals under the command of the doctor Nikolay Pirogov (1810–1881) – a key figure in the introduction of anaesthesia – Nightingale organised a group of nurses to improve the sanitary conditions of the British military hospital of Scutari. Dunant describes Nightingale as a female pioneer in the history of care who, furthermore, contributed to the expansion of humanitarian sensibility.

> Miss Florence Nightingale, who was familiar with the hospitals in England and the principal charitable and philanthropic establishments on the Continent, and who had given up the pleasures of opulence in order to devote herself to doing good, received a pressing appeal from Lord Sidney Herbert, Secretary of War of the British Empire, asking her to go and look after the English soldiers in the Near East (. . .) She left for Constantinople and Scutari in November, 1854, with thirty-seven English ladies, who (. . .) set to work caring for the many wounded (. . .) All that she accomplished during those long months of sublime self-sacrifice, through her passionate devotion to suffering humanity, is well-known (Dunant 1947, 120)

In Dunant's eyes, Nightingale was not as ignorant as the women of Castiglione, probably because she came from an upper-class family, had received an exquisite education in prestigious institutions such as the Kaiserswerth Deaconess Institute and maintained excellent relations with personalities such as the British Secretary at War, Sidney Herbert. Although Herbert had envisaged the introduction of female nurses in the British army from the outbreak of this armed conflict, the publication of several critical articles in *The Times* – written by the Irish reporter William Howard Russell and the English journalist Thomas Chenery – would precipitate his decision to appoint Nightingale as the chief of a mission in the

Crimea. On the 12th October, an editorial written by Chenery (1854, 7) denounced 'with feelings of anger and indignation' the dramatic conditions of the sick and the wounded due to the British army's obsolete medical services and the lack of devoted sisters of charity who could perform a similar role to that accomplished by the Sisters of Saint Vincent de Paul within the French military. Although British audiences originally felt the Crimean War was a distant conflict, the 'communication revolution' (Hutchinson 1996, 28) brought about by journalism – alongside technological developments such as the telegraph and the steam engine – would bring it nearer than previous ones. This editorial provoked such as wave of solidarity from *The Times*' readers that the newspaper created a fund to gather donations which would financially support Nightingale's mission.

On her arrival at the Scutari hospital in the outskirts of Constantinople, Nightingale noticed that more soldiers were dying more from contagious diseases such as cholera, typhus and dysentery than from war wounds and she accused medical officers of having caused this situation due to their carelessness concerning sanitary conditions. Although nursing was established in Scutari as a female activity performed under the responsibility of experienced men such as military physicians – according to Dunant's dream – Nightingale did not respect their authority, as shown in the following letter addressed to the Colonel Lefroy:

> I do not profess to feel any respect for the military medical profession; any more than for any other race of slaves, of whom they have all the vices and all the virtues, but a strong compassion and a burning desire to see them righted (Nightingale 1997, 275)

Here, Nightingale gendered compassion to show her moral superiority over military physicians to whom she referred with contempt as primitive and cruel people – like the slaves – because of their lack of discipline. To demonstrate her leadership in Scutari, Nightingale (1860, 3) introduced some rules concerning the hospital environment, which aimed to use 'fresh air', 'light', 'warmth', quietness and 'cleanliness' to facilitate the recovery of patients. Material conditions of care included organising a laundry, ventilating and cleaning the main facilities of the hospital and fixing a distance between patients' beds to ensure they could breathe fresh air. Nightingale's nurses also took care of washing patients, dressing their wounds and watching over their diet through the administration of properly cooked food. Although Nightingale (1997, 157) is widely acclaimed for founding modern nursing as a secular profession, she pointed out that the practice of care should be conceived as 'a work of mercy'. As a cardinal Christian virtue, mercy has inspired compassion – for providing assistance to brethren in need – in a myriad of worshipers since the Medieval period. As James Gregory (2022, 16) has shown, in nineteenth century British culture, mercy – conceived as an infused divine form of compassion – was intimately related to activities 'now described as humanitarian or philanthropic'. This was particularly the case for Nightingale's duties in Scutari which appear to be the most perfect expression of the works of mercy 'which every good Christian is expected to perform' in order to feed the hungry, give drink to the thirsty and clothe the naked (Zucconi 2018, 2).

Although Nightingale demonstrated how nursing practices could significantly reduce mortality and morbidity rates – namely through her diagrams which visually revealed the impact of introducing care in hospitals – Western audiences were more impressed by her mediatic image as 'an angel of mercy' (see Figure 2). As Dunant (1947, 159) reminds us, her 'picture (. . .) going in the

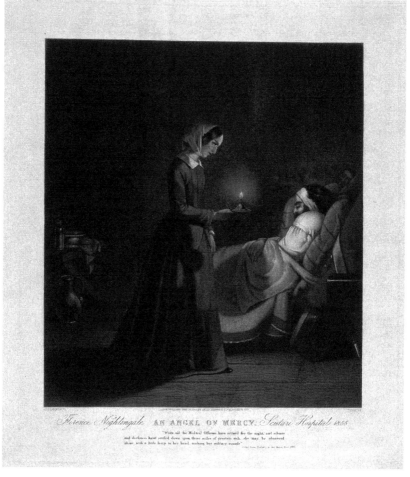

Figure 2 Florence Nightingale. Coloured mezzotint by C.A.Tomkins, 1855, after J. Butterworth. Wellcome Collection. Public Domain

night, with a little lamp in her hand through the immense wards of the military hospital' of Scutari 'will remain imprinted forever in' our 'hearts'. Echoing the mythical representation of Nightingale as the 'lady with the lamp' – which was reproduced for the first time in the *London Illustrated News* on the 24th February 1855 – Dunant (1947, 59) was highlighting values such as 'abnegation', 'holy self-sacrifice' and 'devotion' as quintessential virtues which female relief agents should incarnate in order to take care of the wounded and injured during warfare.

For her part, Nightingale (1860, 200) refused to consider that nurses should just be 'devoted and obedient' – as this definition could also be used to describe a horse's behaviour – but she consciously exploited these allegedly female virtues to justify the inclusion of female nurses into the British military. As she explained in a letter sent from the Crimea on the 9th February 1857 – which probably addressed the British physician John Sutherland – nursing care was a matter of feelings, as it involved the creation of an emotional kinship with soldiers.

> No one can feel for the army as I do. Those people who talk to us have all fed their children on the fat of the land and dressed them in velvet and silk (. . .) I have had to see my children in a dirty blanket and an old pair of regimental trousers, and to see them fed on raw salt meat, and rum and biscuit – and nine thousands of children are lying from causes, which might be prevented, in their forgotten graves. But I can never forget (Nightingale 1997, 294)

Though Nightingale never married and had no children of her own, she introduced herself as the mother of the British army in order to associate compassion with a female disposition which was inspired by the Christian ideal represented by the Virgin Mary within the Biblical tradition. As Katherine Ibbett (2018, 16) has pointed out, the figure of the *Mater Dolorosa* came to symbolise the essential 'compassionate character' in late medieval Europe, 'because of Jesus, after Jesus, she gives birth only to pain'. Coming from the Latin root *pati*, the word 'compassion' – literally meaning 'suffering with' – was specifically embodied by a gendered figure such as the Virgin who played a central role in the Passion of Jesus. Portraying herself as the mother of those British soldiers who had lost their lives in the Crimea – and with whom she had suffered their sorrows in her flesh – Nightingale was emulating the Virgin mother as she mourned her son following his crucifixion. In doing so she was not merely giving voice to her religious sentiments, but – more importantly – she was providing a model for future generations of nurses which could regulate their moral behaviour through values such as chastity, so as to preserve their female honour. Gender stereotypes – such as the representation of female nurses as compassionate mothers – ensured that respectable ladies could carefully distinguish themselves from working-class women who had traditionally performed caring activities but who were associated with alcoholics and prostitutes in Victorian culture. Nightingale's model was intended to control female nurses' sexualities by avoiding any form of carnal love with patients, bringing into focus the extent to which women of ill repute were considered to be the main cause of the spread of venereal diseases such as syphilis.

Maternal feelings – linked to love, compassion and sympathy – also allowed Nightingale to impose the moral superiority of her own model of nursing over other cultures of care promoted during the Crimean War, such as that represented by the British-Jamaican healer Mary Seacole (1805–1881) who introduced the use of the herbal remedies which she had learnt from Afro-Caribbean traditions. Although Seacole initially expected to join Nightingale's mission in Scutari, she was rejected because her creole ancestry did not embody the Britishness of the Empire. Therefore, she decided to finance her own expedition to set up her 'British hotel' in Balaclava (Seacole 2005, 47). As a representative of 'maternal imperialism' (Ramusack 1992, 119), Nightingale did not accept Seacole as a loyal colonial subject, as she could not contemplate the participation of women who did not fit with Queen Victoria's symbolic representation as the Great White Queen.

Despite the uncontested humanitarian spirit which Dunant bestowed on Nightingale during the Crimean War, she had only been performing her duty as a nurse belonging to a national army. This perspective provided her with a privileged position for formulating one of the most critical objections to the creation of the ICRC. In a letter addressed to the British military physician Thomas Longmore – who attended the 1864 Geneva Conference – Nightingale (1864, 7–8) considered the organisation of 'a voluntary international system' to relieve the wounded as an 'absurd project', which could only have been imagined 'in a little state, like Geneva' that was spared from the pain of warfare. For her, accepting the 'voluntary effort' suggested by Dunant would only weaken 'the military character' of the medical services, 'unless such effort were to become military in its organisation'. Despite Nightingale's initial scepticism towards this humanitarian agency, her compassionate figure holding a little lamp remains the iconic representation of female relief agents within this movement right up to the present day, as shown by the highest award conferred on Red Cross nurses: the Florence Nightingale Medal.

2.2 Compassion in Conflict

In the aftermath of the Franco-Prussian War, Nightingale (1872) wrote a letter to Dunant in which she radically changed her tone towards ICRC representatives, as she recognised the success of their initiative and accepted to attach 'her poor name to this great work', as a way 'to acknowledge the manner in which all the English women (...) had worked under' its 'auspices during the last war'. As Nightingale pointed out, the Franco-Prussian War – a conflict which had been declared by Napoleon III's French Empire against Otto Bismarck's Kingdom of Prussia – tested, under fire, the compassion of a heterogonous group of female nurses and volunteers who had joined national Red Cross societies, as well as a myriad of charitable initiatives which supported the creation of a plethora of field hospitals. British women, such as the nurses Emma Maria Pearson (1828–1893) and Louisa MacLaughlin (1836–1921) first joined the Anglo-American ambulance after the Battle of Sedan and, later on, organised an ambulance of their own which they financed through donations received from *The Times*' readers (Pearson and MacLaughlin 1871). This conflict also gave French women the opportunity to proudly wear the Red Cross emblem, such as the actress Sarah Bernhardt (1844–1923) who ran an ambulance at the Théatre de l'Odéon during the siege of Paris and the Protestant philanthropist Sarah Monod (1836–1912) who was the head of female Deaconesses in the Evangelic ambulance. Nursing did not just allow British and French women to practice their citizenship in this war context (Taithe 2001, 27–8), this was also the case for other European women who regarded humanitarian work as a field which could provide them with a certain sense of emancipation, even though this was through conservative gender roles.

For instance, the Belgian Baroness Ida de Crombrugghe (1820–1875), a prominent philanthropist who also struggled for women's right to education, played a central role in the creation of a ladies' committee under the auspices of the Belgian Red Cross. By launching this initiative concurrently with King Leopold II's mobilisation of the Belgian army on the frontiers of Belgium's territory, Crombrugghe showed that compassion could also be organised in a military fashion in order to protect the political interests of a neutral country across its national borders. Crombrugghe departed from Brussels with a group of volunteer nurses in order to support the Prussian Society for the Relief of Wounded Soldiers. On her arrival at the field hospital of Sarrebruck, Crombrugghe explained in her diary that she had just received a letter from a friend, who was also a volunteer nurse during this conflict. Her friend's confessions provided Crombrugghe with the occasion to recreate the literary representation of the nurse as a modern Madonna by echoing the performative effects that compassion had within the Biblical tradition.

> The doctor Heine entrusted me with the operation room. This task is arduous [...]. However, I feel like a mother who would rather see her child suffer under her own eyes than to entrust them to a stranger. Is this poor soldier not already relieved to see someone who sympathises with his suffering? (Crombrugghe 1871, 23)

Crombrugghe's practice of diary writing allowed her to craft her intimate self in the light of Nightingale's founding myth, by regarding soldiers as Christian martyrs who were dying – under the symbol of the cross – to save their motherland, as Jesus had done previously in the name of the whole of mankind. By re-enacting a traditional vision of femininity – which put the accent on its natural compassionate character – Crombrugghe was, nevertheless, carving out a space for women's participation in international politics during a period in which women had no formal rights as citizens. Although Crombrugghe was expected to remain neutral, she did not hide her sympathies for Prussia when she denounced France's long imperial history. Remembering Napoleon Bonaparte's invasion of the Belgian territory, Crombrugghe (1871, 162) complained about the brutalisation of Prussians in French propaganda as 'Germany' actually signified 'the progress of modern science', as well as the highest expression of civilisation through the works of 'Kant, Schiller and Goethe'. Through her words, Crombrugghe's compassion towards Prussia appears to have been a way for her to exercise her patriotism for her country. As a representative of a neutral state, Crombrugghe's Red Cross ladies' committee can, therefore, be understood as a key female contribution to the war effort which aimed to calm Napoleon III's ambition of annexing Belgium to the French Empire. The blurring of frontiers between humanitarian compassion and politics would become even more confused during the First World War, when national Red Cross societies were instrumentalised by governments to instil a sense of nationalism amongst voluntary female nurses.

In 1914, another female representative of a small, neutral, Central European country – Switzerland – received nursing training before joining the hospital 101 in Lyon which had been set up in an old veterinary school to assist wounded French soldiers during the Great War. The Genevan journalist and novelist Hélène Pittard-Dufour (1874–1953) – better known by her literary pseudonym Noëlle Roger (1991, 1) – is said to have decided to do this because she felt 'no longer able to be interested in the subjects linked to fiction writing that had absorbed [her] up until then'. In spite of this, Roger was a prolific writer during wartime and recorded her experiences in various notebooks which she used for her later publications – all of which were destined to celebrate the humanitarian involvement of the Helvetic Confederation. The first to appear in a series of fascicles was *Les carnets d'une infirmière* [The notebooks of a nurse]. In its preface, Roger (1915a, 7–9) explains to her readers: 'this is nothing but a lowly diary', 'the testimony' of a friend, who also worked as a Red Cross nurse before dying from an 'infectious flu'. Roger did not only dedicate her publication to her colleague – a 'war martyr' – but also to 'the mothers of France' in order to 'glorify the spirit of French soldiers' who became, thus, the main recipient of compassion in Roger's narrative. However, her war notebooks demonstrate that her manuscript was probably inspired by her own experience, which she consciously masked under the literary figure of an unknown nurse. Whether or not the main character is real, or just a product of Roger's imagination, this narrative provides a rich example for exploring how Swiss women actively participated as humanitarian agents during the First World War. As Belgian women did during the Franco-Prussian War, Swiss women joined the flourishing industry of humanitarian work which exploited a particular form of made-in-Helvetia compassion with a twofold purpose: preventing the invasion of its territory and providing a feeling of national unity within this country which – as already explained – was confronted by its population's different political affinities.

In *Les carnets d'un témoin* [The notebooks of a witness], Roger explicitly associates Swiss patriotism with the compassionate character of this country when she describes the humanitarian hospital-train operation organised by the ICRC in collaboration with the SRC, which was under the direction of the Swiss army. This mission ensured the exchange of seriously wounded French and German soldiers who had been imprisoned using hospital-trains which circulated through Swiss territory under the responsibility of Karl and Mary Bohny – the SRC' chief medical officer and the superintendent of female nurses, respectively. The transit of these trains raised so much expectation that Swiss people welcomed soldiers with all sorts of offerings at the country's main train stations. When 'the train arrives at the station' – Roger wrote – it was 'preceded by an immense clamour'. Swiss nurses were also waiting for soldiers on the platform. Soldiers addressed another of Roger's fictional nurses in the following terms: 'Madame, we follow you as if you were our mother!' Roger (1915b, 110) celebrated this type of collective performance of compassion to consecrate Swiss people as the champions of charity during warfare. Furthermore, her publications also allow us to recognise the legacy of Nightingale's model as they specifically represent care as a sort of spiritual conversion, which required not only the discipline of keeping a diary, but also that of wearing a nurse's uniform.

> Suddenly, personality fades under the uniform. You only feel an immense desire to do good, the absolute consent of your whole self to discipline. You become that anonymous being who obeys the sound of a bell, the doctor's gesture, the patient's call, who stands respectfully at the head of the bed (Roger 1915a, 15)

In Roger's words, the representation of female relief agents as compassionate mothers who were destined to comfort soldiers' suffering reaches its paroxysm, as it led her to feel like a virgin. Uniforms, the design of which were inspired by nuns' habits and veils, appeared as a key textile element for successfully performing a caring relationship with men as they proved nurses' asexual devotion (Darrow 1996, 90). However, for many volunteers, taking care of convalescent soldiers involved – in practice – the discovery of male bodies in all their nudity. Thus, Roger recreated the scene in which she contemplated a young wounded soldier's body as a moment full of aesthetic pleasure, showing the intimate connections working between female compassion and sexual desire in the light of a 'pornography of pain', which has been an 'integral part of the humanitarian sensibility' since its beginnings (Halttunen 1995, 304).

> A lean and muscular body, the ribs drawn very clearly, raising the skin, the chest filled with a large wound with a drain emerging from it [...] I made out the face, a narrow forehead under the brush cut hair, two very dark eyebrows [...] He too, with his thin body, pierced chest and dark oval face, made me think of a painting by the Flemish Primitives: a martyr subdued by atrocious suffering (Roger 1915a, 25)

As described by voluntary nurses – including Crombrugghe and Roger – in their writings, their compassion economy appeared to be related to an ideal of humanity which sacralised soldiers' pain through the Christian image of the martyr who died for their mother country. Deeply inspired by Nightingale's model, they demonstrated the perfect appropriation of the Red Cross' emotional orthodoxy. Even though Crombrugghe and Roger belonged to neutral countries, humanitarianism became a way for them to show their patriotism. Although the association of women with compassion enabled these upper-class, Christian and white women to participate in warfare within the framework of an 'Imperial feminism' (Burton 1994, 2), it also reified the gender stereotypes which have overshadowed their capital contribution to the history of international health.

3 Experiences during the Long Second World War

One of the main objectives of the history of emotions has been to abolish any dichotomy between affective, sensitive and rational phenomena in the study of the past. However – throughout the completion of my project – I remarked that the use of the term 'emotion' as a historical category was reinforcing the divisions which emotion history was originally intended to combat. Furthermore – as my fellow historians working at the University of Geneva warned me – the use of emotion as a category of inquiry is not the best methodological choice for avoiding presentist interpretations of the past, because our comprehension of emotions remains extremely close to the meaning that they have acquired in evolutionary psychology (Boddice 2019, 188). In this section, I turn to the new history of experiences (Boddice and Smith 2020; Kivimaäki et al. 2021; Nagy and Biron-Ouellet 2020 and 2022) to examine how emotions, senses and memories are interconnected 'aspects of human experience' (Eyice 2021, 301) which allow us to explore models of femininity that differ from the archetypal representation promoted by the Red Cross. But in making this choice, I am not assuming that 'experience' is a category of inquiry which involves less serious theoretical challenges.

As Joan W. Scott (1991, 776) reminds us, 'experience' is a category which has usually been taken for granted by gender historians who analyse documents such as autobiographies, as this type of material does not necessarily provide us with factual evidence about what has happened. Although these sources give us an impression of authenticity, historians should remain cautious because this kind of narrative can contribute to naturalising the ideologies they are looking to deconstruct, including that of sexual difference. To prevent the reproduction of preconceived social identities, Scott suggests approaching the notion of 'experience' as a social construction which should be contextualised within gender, class, racial and religious power relations. While I acknowledge the benefits of mobilising Scott's intersectional approach, this perspective also reveals its limitations because – under these theoretical lenses – women humanitarians' experiences are judged as and reduced to simple instruments of the regimes of power. In fact, Scott (1991, 797) concludes in her article that 'it is tempting to abandon the notion of experience', as it is a mere linguistic reality which only serves to 'essentialise identity and reify the subject'. From Scott's view, it follows that the only authentic experience which we have the right to feel as individuals is that of our own deconstruction in the light of the structures of power under which we have been modulated. However, this conclusion implies an extremely frustrating experience, as it leaves no room for either the agency of the subject under study or our own as historians.

My contention of Scott's critique echoes the research conducted by historians who have highlighted the potentialities of experience as a category which enables the study of 'the ways in which living was real in historical terms' including 'practice, sensation, feeling, emotion and thought' (Boddice and Smith 2020, 23), as well as its relations with 'memory and imagination' (Nagy and Biron-Ouellet 2022, 6). By engaging with the 'tools and the concepts' that historians of emotions and the senses 'have developed over the past thirty years' (Hoegaerts and Olsen 2021, 376), the history of experiences appears to be a fruitful approach for challenging the idea that this reality exclusively belongs to individual subjects. As Salaria Kea and Elisabeth Eidenbenz's stories demonstrate, experiences can be understood as a coproduction involving various actors who have reshaped them according to their unresolved resentments and long-lasting hopes for claiming justice for the victims of mass atrocities. Indeed, these case studies have become meaningful experiences for me, because they have radically changed my own way of thinking, feeling and doing history.

3.1 Black Resentment and All That Jazz

Despite its influence, not all female aid workers were trained in the 'school of emotions' federated by the Red Cross movement. This was mainly because certain women did not meet the Red Cross' gender, class and racial expectations and, therefore, did not vocalise its rules and 'translate them into personal attitudes and conduct' (Frevert 2011, 14). One of the most stimulating cases that I have ever studied – because it challenges many Western stereotypes about what a woman humanitarian should look like – is that of Kea. Her story is a rare one, which denounces to what extent racial discrimination has been an integral part of the Western humanitarian system since its early beginnings. Like Seacole, Kea had to overcome manifold obstacles to become a nurse and, later on, an international volunteer. Born on the 13th July 1913 in Milledgeville – Georgia – and raised in Akron – Ohio – by several foster families, she moved to New York City in the 1930s because Harlem Hospital offered one of the few nursing training programs that accepted Afro-American students. However, Kea soon realised to what extent racial segregation regulated the daily life of this hospital when she was forbidden to sit in a part of the dining room which was reserved for white staff. This led Kea (1938, 5, undated a, 8) to organise a protest together with other Afro-American nurses, but this would not be the last time that she suffered social exclusion because of her racial origins. When she tried to join the American Red Cross in 1936, to help victims affected by the floods that had devastated Ohio and Kentucky, her application was declined because of the colour of her skin. Even though the American Red Cross was founded in 1882 by the women's rights activist Clara Barton (1821–1912), Black nurses were barred from serving in this institution except in some exceptional cases, such as the 1918 influenza pandemic. Therefore, Kea turned her interest towards other initiatives led by Afro-American activists and founded a committee in Harlem to raise funds to send medical supplies to support Ethiopia; a nation which, at that time, was being attacked by Benito Mussolini. Shortly after this, the Spanish Civil War broke out and Kea joined the American Medical Bureau (hereafter AMB). This was an amalgam of grass-roots leftist groups which denounced the Neutrality Law adopted by the United States in 1937 and only provided humanitarian relief to the Second Spanish Republic.[9] Kea's engagement in this mission illustrates

---

[9] The AMB included Communists, Afro-Americans and Jews, but not exclusively as shown by the Unitarian religious convictions of the North-American physician Walter B. Cannon, its chair from 1937 to 1939. See Arrizabalaga and Martínez-Vidal (2022).

a culture of humanitarianism which has nothing to do with impartiality, neutrality or independence, as these principles 'do not help the victims of crimes against humanity' (Barnett 2014, 244). During the Second World War, Kea volunteered in the United States Army Nurse Corps – which for the first time accepted Afro-American nurses amongst its ranks – and assisted wounded soldiers in France.

Moreover, Kea's story is mesmerising because it provides a controversial historical case for scholars who are willing to recover the experiences of marginal voices by analysing sources such as autobiographies, biographies, oral records and documentaries. When I started conducting research on Kea, I first consulted her autobiographical account *While Passing Through* (Kea undated a), as well as an untitled typescript memoir (Kea undated b). This was partially published in 1938 as *A Negro Nurse in Republican Spain*; however, these manuscripts reveal several differences. For example, *While Passing Through* finishes at the end of the Spanish Civil War, whereas *A Negro Nurse* concludes when Kea was still raising funds to help the Spanish Republic. What was more intriguing though was that these manuscripts revealed several contradictions with Kea's oral records. While, in *A Negro Nurse*, she explained that her father – who was a gardener in a sanatorium – was killed by a patient (Kea 1938, 4), in an interview that she gave to the oral historian John Gerassi at the end of her life, she insisted that her father was a sailor who died during the First World War (Kea 1980). This was not the only disturbing detail in Kea's accounts. In *A Negro Nurse*, Kea (1938, 7) joined the second medical unit that the AMB sent to Spain, whereas official photographs reveal that she departed from New York abroad *The Paris* with the third medical mission launched by this organisation on the 27th March 1937. Furthermore, in Gerassi's interview, Kea evoked that she had been captured by German soldiers in Spain, but in *A Negro Nurse* there is only the mention of the fact that she got lost on the Front of Teruel (Kea 1938, 13).

All these inconsistencies led the American feminist writer Frances Patai (1990) to conclude that 'Salaria may have confused fact with fiction.' Besides Patai, Fredericka Martin – chief nurse of the AMB – also questioned the accuracy of several passages of Kea's *While Passing Through* (Everly 2022a, 8). The exchanges which I have maintained with the American filmmaker Julia Newman – director of *Into the Fire: American Women during the Spanish Civil War* (2002) – led me to realise that Kea suffered from a form of dementia at the end of her life. Therefore, I concluded during my research stay in New York that Kea's testimonies were more intended to create a political myth representing the Negro Committee than to account for her real humanitarian experience in Spain (Martín-Moruno 2016b, 6). Although at that time there had not been any comprehensive study focused on Kea's accounts, since then other researchers have provided new perspectives for interpreting these materials. For instance, Cañete Quesada (2019, 115–16) has pointed out that what is interesting in all these divergent narratives is recovering Kea's 'under-represented voice as a part of a collective marginalized group', rather than determining their 'level of objectivity' or 'ascertaining the total and absolute truth about the war'. For her part, Anne Donlon (2019) has argued that *A Negro Nurse* was composed by the Afro-American activist Thyra Johnson Edwards (1897–1953): Kea's fellow volunteer in Spain who, later on, toured the United States with her to raise funds for the Spanish Republic. As Emily Robins Sharpe (2020, 92) has suggested, it does not matter if this manuscript was not actually written by Kea, as it remains a crucial document for examining what has been censored by later commentators. More recently, Kathryn Everly (2022a) has moved this line of research forward by showing that Kea's own words were frequently discredited in order to hide the racism of North-American leftists and, therefore, offer an idyllic vision of the AMB as an organisation which 'transcended racial, ethnic, religious, class and gender stereotypes' (Patai 1990, 80). For Everly (2022a, 1), the 'textual violence exerted' by those who have commented on Kea's life allows us 'to have a sense of what her experience may have been like'.

The work conducted by all of these scholars has led me to realise to what extent I was completely unfair to Kea when I judged that her testimonies did not provide an accurate representation of her experiences. Although the instability of Kea's shifting memories has been largely attributed to the Alzheimer's disease that she suffered from, her divergent memories also tell us something about how historians should approach the experiences of individuals who make up part of their investigations. Rather than being material which can be simply judged as being true or false, Kea's floating experiences should be considered as an imaginative negotiation between Kea herself and her contemporaries – Johnson Edwards and Martin – as well as with future researchers who have been active agents in the trial of these experiences during the twentieth and twenty-first centuries. From this approach, Kea's testimonies can be regarded as excellent material for examining the collective production of a model of humanitarian action which emerged as the female counterpart of the New Negro Man: the ideal of the Afro-American activist who defended his rights during the 1930s Harlem Renaissance.

In *A Negro Nurse*, its author – either Kea or Johnson Edwards, or both of them as female representatives of the Negro Committee to Aid Spanish Democracy – provides some key elements for understanding why Afro-Americans felt committed to aiding Spanish Republicans in a fratricidal war which was taking place far away from the United States.

> What have the Negroes to do with Spain? (. . .) What about Ethiopia? (. . .)
> These are the questions Negroes are constantly asking (. . .) Quite apart from
> the broad question of humanitarianism the answers are simple. Fascist Italy

invaded and overpowered Ethiopia. This was a terrible blow to negroes throughout the world. Ethiopia represented the last outpost of (. . .) Negro self-government (. . .) Italy moved on from the invasion of Ethiopia. She advanced her troops into Spain (. . .) Bitter resentment against Italy still rankled. The hundreds of Negro boys who had been prevented from going to Ethiopia understood the issues more clearly now (. . .) Ethiopia's only hope for recovery lies in Italy's defeat. The place to defeat Italy just now is Spain (Kea 1938, 3)

As explained in *A Negro Nurse*, Afro-Americans joined the International Brigades as regular fighters, because they interpreted the Spanish Civil War as the continuation of the Italian invasion of Ethiopia: the emblem of Africa's resistance against Western colonial powers since its victory over the Italian army during the First Italo-Ethiopian war (1895–1896). Ethiopia had been transformed into a vibrant cultural symbol by Afro-American artists, writers and jazz musicians belonging to the Harlem Renaissance, who celebrated the last uncolonised African nation. Sculptures such as Loïs Mailou Jones' *The Ascent of Ethiopia* (1932) or poems such as Langston Hughes' *Call for Ethiopia* (1994, 184) show to what extent Haile Selassie's Kingdom of Ethiopia came to be an emotional site from which the Afro-American community retraced their racial identity through their diaspora and enslavement, as well as their expectations about their future emancipation from Western Imperialism. This explains why Black people around the world suffered – what the author of *A Negro Nurse* termed – a 'terrible blow' after Mussolini's aggression. In this narrative, the suffering of Ethiopians operated like a kind of mirror which shed light on the pain experienced by Afro-Americans and, later, on that endured by Republican Spaniards who became Mussolini's new target when he supported Nationalist troops in Spain. Thus, the involvement of Afro-Americans in the Spanish Civil War could be explained through – what the late–eighteenth century Scottish moral philosopher Adam Smith (1767, 46) referred to as – sympathy: 'the fellow-feeling with the suffering of others' who are familiar to us. However, Kea did not represent the impartial spectator – imagined by Smith – but rather a partisan one. By identifying a common transnational politics of hate represented by supremacist groups such as the Ku Klux Klan in the United States, the 'Rome-Berlin-Tokyo axis' and Francoist Spain, Kea (undated a, 12) widened her familiar scope of sympathy to embrace all those who were being discriminated against during the long Second World War, whether they were Afro-Americans, Ethiopians, Spanish Republicans or Jews.

Paraphrasing Kea's words, 'the lynching of Negroes in most cities and very poor ones in others, all this appeared to them as a part of the picture of fascism'. For Kea (1938, 3), fascism was an ideology that always involved 'a dominant group impoverishing and degrading a less powerful'. In Spain, Kea (1938, 8) acknowledged that she had discovered 'the first example of discrimination where race was not a factor', as the battle that was being fought there confronted 'peasantry versus nobility'. However, the dramatic conditions under which Spanish peasants were living resembled, in many ways, those that Afro-Americans were suffering from in the United States. Although Spanish 'peasants had previously accepted the belief that nothing could be done' for them – like the Harlem hospital's Afro-American nurses – Kea was fully convinced that they should resist and fight, because 'liberty could be a reality'. As Kea (1938, 8) foresaw, 'there was nothing inviolable about the old prejudices', as 'they could be changed and justice established'. Within her humanitarianism, nursing care became a political weapon which channelled a 'bitter feeling of resentment' against those who perpetrated crimes against humanity. Unlike indignation, resentment 'cannot be fully gratified, unless the offender' grieves 'in his turn (...) for that particular wrong which we have suffered from him' (Smith 1767, 75). As a type of desire for revenge, resentment became a key emotion for interpreting why the Afro-American community felt the imperious need to help Republican Spain: because defeating Italy in Spain represented 'the only hope for Ethiopia's recovery' (Kea 1938, 3). Rather than introducing resentment as a pathological emotion in the light of Nietzsche's *ressentiment* (*ressentiment* is a generalised resentment against social groups, rather than individuals), *A Negro Nurse* echoes the creative affective force which this 'ugly feeling' (Ngai 2005, 33–4) had acquired within the emotional repertoire of the Harlem Renaissance to restore the dignity of Afro-Americans. Representing a group which was a racial minority within the AMB, Kea's humanitarianism appeared, therefore, as a manner to struggle for justice by supporting the punishment of those groups who had perpetrated crimes against humanity. Thus, in *A Negro Nurse*, resentment looks more like a virtue which should be cultivated by those who resist forgetting and forgiving their past injuries until justice can be done (Brudholm 2008, 6). Under the lenses of this emotion, it appears that Kea's humanitarianism was not exclusively oriented to palliating the symptoms of warfare. Using Michael Barnett's terminology (2011, 37–8), Kea contributed to the development of an 'alchemical humanitarianism' which sought to eliminate the root causes of suffering and, unlike 'emergency humanitarianism', evolved in relation to the advocacy of a human-rights agenda that went well beyond the mere objective of saving lives.

Although Kea's voice performed the values supported by the Afro-American community, her testimonies also provide some elements which contribute to shedding light on her personal experiences as the only Negro female nurse who joined the AMB. For instance, in *While Passing Through*, it is said that 'many people visited and remarked the lone Negro-girl serving so diligently yet so far was she from any women of her kind' (Kea undated b, 26). Kea probably felt alone because she did not fit with the gender stereotypes which represented white female volunteers within the AMB as 'angels of the last pure war' (Green, 1977). As Langston Hughes (1964, 382) wrote in his autobiography: 'when I met her at Villa Paz', she had just become 'Mr. John Joseph O'Reilly's wife' when she married an Irish ambulance driver belonging to the International Brigades. Although in *A Negro Nurse* there is no mention of O'Reilly, Kea married him on the 2nd October 1937. By marrying a white man, Kea was not only breaking with the ideal of femininity represented by Nightingale's model of nurses as women who should sublimate their sexuality in the service of humanity, she was also challenging the colonial discourse on love which exerted strong discrimination on mixed-race couples in the United States. Though Kea (undated b, 33) was initially reluctant to get engaged to a white man, she and O'Reilly would remain together until the end of their lives, because loving each other was the best way to 'abolish the enemies of the human race'. For them, love was the result of their shared political beliefs in a vision of humanity free from all forms of discrimination. In *A Negro Nurse*, this new religion of humanity is associated with the international volunteers who were convalescents at the American hospital at Villa Paz, who formed a community of feeling while sharing their hopes in the promise of a fairer future world.

> The hospital beds were soon filled with soldiers (. . .) Czechs (. . .), French, Finns (. . .) Germans and Italians, exiled or escaped from concentration camps (. . .) Ethiopians (. . .) Cubans, Mexicans, Russians (. . .) and Japanese, unsympathetic with Japan's invasion of China (. . .) These divisions of race (. . .), religion and nationality lost significance when they met in Spain in a united effort to make Spain the tomb of fascism. The outcome of the struggle in Spain implies the (. . .) realisation of the hopes of the minorities of the world (Kea 1938, 6)

In Kea's narrative, hope became a central motive which allows us to acknowledge the strong spiritual dimension of her humanitarian engagement. Halfway between secular and messianic traditions, Kea's hope was fuelled by the Marxist utopia which had been widely spread by Communist groups in the United States – such as the AMB – as well as by Black Christianity – which identified Ethiopia with Egypt in the biblical verses of the Psalms. Kea was a figure who embraced both traditions, even though she remained ambivalent towards her communist affiliation. Although she joined the Communist party in 1935, she explained at the end of her life that 'she did not even know what a Communist was (. . .)' as she 'thought that it was for white people only, like the Mafia' (Byrne 2007, 79). Kea's religious beliefs were not mentioned either in

A Negro Nurse. However, in another autobiographical manuscript, which she entitled *May Every Knock Be a Boost* and *Hope*, she openly recognises that her spiritual quest shaped her vocation as an international nurse. As Kea (undated b, 8, undated c, 1) wrote, 'my hope was to become a nurse' (. . .) 'some call' this spirituality 'Christianity', others 'adventure' or just 'humanitarianism'.

Far from romance, Kea's wartime experience was marked by the fear of constant bombardments. First, her medical unit was attacked at Villa Paz and, later on, in La Puebla de Híjar, a town belonging to the province of Teruel, where the bombs 'wounded Helen Freeman, an American nurse' (Kea 1938, 12). When Kea arrived in Barcelona – a city which was 'under continual bombardment' – she witnessed the attack of several colonies for refugee children. There, Kea (1938, 13) described the stench of death, while she and other nurses 'gathered up the broken fragments of human bodies – brains, limbs (. . .) a section of head'. In the end, Kea (1938, 14) herself was injured by an explosion, 'when her hospital unit suffered a bombardment'. *A Negro Nurse* described the end of Kea's humanitarian experiences, by stating that she recovered in a hospital in France before returning to New York, where she continued to raise funds for the Spanish cause, moved by the hope represented by the battle which Afro-Americans were fighting in Spain.

Alongside the brave Afro-American soldiers who volunteered in the International Brigades, Kea's engagement has been recently interpreted as the foundations of a female model of 'Black feminist solidarity' (Everly 2022b). This shows to what extent the negotiation of her experiences is still in the making. Although Kea has come to represent a culture of humanitarianism symbolising the Afro-American community, she was reluctant to exclusively define her citizen activism through her racial origins. Despite conceiving her nursing care as being intimately linked to her struggle against white supremacy, the Spanish Civil War led Kea to discover that her beliefs in a shared humanity went well beyond any such distinction; especially when she fell in love with O'Reilly, the man who made her feel 'like a natural woman' (Butler 1990, 212).[10] In the end, a history of experiences approach enables us to acknowledge that Kea's testimonies do not tell us anything that can be considered as true or fiction, even though she suffered from a type of dementia. Instead, they tell us something about what it meant to feel like a human whose humanity had not been fully recognised because of the triple discrimination she faced as a woman, a working-class activist and an Afro-American.

---

[10] Butler uses Aretha Franklin's song *(You Make Me Feel Like) A Natural Woman* (1967) to introduce her notion of gender as being fluid, rather than a fixed substance.

3.2 Remembering Experiences

Doing oral history can become an addictive experience, as it provides historians with a unique opportunity to engage in a conversation with actors who have lived – what is considered to be – a significant past. In my case, oral history has given me the privilege of going deeper into the story of the Swiss relief worker Elisabeth Eidenbenz through the memories of one of her beneficiaries, Guy Eckstein: an eighty-one-year-old Belgian and also naturalised Swiss citizen, who currently lives in Geneva. Remembering Eidenbenz's humanitarian experiences throughout the long Second World War, we have produced histories together which go well beyond the information preserved in the archives. Eckstein's archive of his own includes not only his memories, but also private letters that he exchanged with Eidenbenz, newspaper clippings, audio recordings, documentary films, photographs and physical objects. These multifarious materials have enlivened our conversations by allowing us to visualise, hear, touch and, even, smell and taste Eidenbenz's story – namely by remembering her love for chocolate.

As a practice, oral history demonstrates that experiences are not merely what is perceived as immediate by an individual – something that is described in German with the term '*Erlebnis*', which is frequently translated into English as 'lived experience' (Jay 2005, 22). This is because experiences are also 'social processes' which involve an intersubjective negotiation between the individual subject who tests his 'own understanding' against 'other people's explanations' (Katajala-Peltomaa and Toivo 2022). In this sense, experiences do not only refer to the feeling of a discrete moment, they also imply adopting the necessary epistemic distance to evaluate what we have lived – as described by the German term '*Erfahrung*'. Resulting from the combination of the verb '*fahren*' (to travel) with the prefix '*er*' that indicates its successful conclusion, the term '*Erfahrung*' highlights that experiences are also associated with the 'learning process' our life journey encompasses (Jay 2005, 22). Last but not least, for certain communities, experiences can become 'social structures' which determine how people can successfully deal with others in the world. In this alchemical transformation of experiences into models of knowing, feeling and interacting, 'shared memories of past experiences' play a central role, as they shape both our 'present interpretations' and 'future expectations' (Katajala-Peltomaa and Toivo 2022). As experiences that are remembered – and, therefore, selected – memories constitute legitimate sources for historians who are willing to investigate how the past has circulated across generations and, thus, formed different communities of feeling when these memories have been actualised through their reception.

The oral history project which I have conducted with Eckstein reveals the formation of historical experiences as successive geological strata particularly well. While remembering Eidenbenz's story with Eckstein, I realised that I was not just reconstructing what she actually said she had lived, but also the negotiation of her experiences with Eckstein at the end of her life, as well as those with various 'trauma communities' (Leese 2022, 6) – including Spanish Republicans, Catalonians, Holocaust survivors and LGBT activists. Such disparate groups have, thus, turned Eidenbenz into an iconic humanitarian figure which has undergone constant political revision during the twenty-first century. Eckstein (2017) is perfectly aware of the various – and, even, competing – political appropriations of Eidenbenz's story, as he has actively contributed to making her humanitarian work known 'so that it can be used as an example for future generations'. The relevance of his testimony is that, despite Eckstein's Jewish origins, he does not profess the Jewish faith and remains very critical about current political uses of the Holocaust. Therefore, his voice represents a powerful 'deviation of narrative states' (Leese 2022, 26) which echoes 'the human condition' that Hannah Arendt (1958) put at the centre of her thinking: the figure of the pariah. Arendt – who herself was a refugee during Second World War – considered the pariah as the outsider of history who proudly felt their '*in*authenticity' (Boddice 2022) within the rules represented by the Jewish establishment.

As Eckstein has explained to me, he met Eidenbenz for the first time in the maternity home which she had set up in an old chateau in Elne – a village close to Perpignan – when he was born on the 10th October 1941. Naturally, Eckstein cannot remember this moment, but Eidenbenz took care to immortalise his presence at the home by taking a photograph of him – as she did for many children born in Elne's maternity (see Figure 3). At that time, Eidenbenz worked for the Schweizerische Arbeitsgemeinschaft für Kriegsgeschädigte Kinder (Swiss Aid to Child Victims of War organisation) which resulted from the merger of several Swiss associations inspired by protestant, pacifist and moderate leftist ideals (Martín-Moruno 2020c, 486). From 1942 – when Germans occupied Vichy France – the Swiss Federal Council issued the ruling that this organisation should work under the auspices of the SRC and, therefore, it was renamed the Schweizerisches Rotes Kreuz/Kinderhilfe (SRC/Aid to Children organisation).

Eidenbenz assisted Eckstein's mother in giving birth when she was a young humanitarian volunteer, aged twenty-eight years. However, this was not her first experience assisting displaced populations. She had previously worked for the Schweizerische Arbeitsgemeinschaft für Spanienkinder (Swiss Aid to Spanish Children organisation): the name under which this humanitarian agency had

Figure 3 'Guy'. Fonds Elisabeth Eidenbenz –Ville d'Elne.
Copyright, all rights reserved

already operated during the Spanish Civil War. Throughout this conflict, she took care of children who had been evacuated from Republican zones due to the bombardments perpetrated by the insurgents in collaboration with German and Italian air forces. Eidenbenz (1938a) was in charge of providing milk to children in the Swiss aid organisation's operational base in Burjassot; a village situated in the south-eastern region of Valencia. She also had the opportunity to work in Madrid, where Swiss canteens were located in former Protestant schools such as 'El Porvenir' and 'Esperanza' (Eidenbenz 1938b). Literally meaning future and hope, these refuges did not just aim to feed elderly persons, children and their mother, but also to emotionally support the people of Madrid during the siege of the capital when it remained encircled by the insurgent forces from November 1936 until the end of the war.

Eidenbenz remained active in Spain until the fall of Barcelona. However, she had predicted with anxiety some months before – what she interpreted as – the beginning of another war in which European democracies would be forced to 'fight for [their] own freedom' (Eidenbenz 1938c). After the exodus of around half a million Republicans across the French border, she assisted pregnant Spanish women who had been resettled in improvised camps in the French Rousillon – such as that of Argèles-sur-Mer – following Édouard Daladier's Decree-Law concerning undesirable foreigners. Eidenbenz first set up a maternity in Brouilla and then, in 1939, she opened that of Elne. From June 1940, she provided medical care not only to pregnant Spanish Republican women, but also to pregnant Jewish women of various nationalities who were living without any sanitary conditions in camps such as that of Rivesaltes.

What is surprising is that Eckstein's mother – Henrika Kone – was not interned in a camp. As Eckstein has clarified for me, she and his father – Moszech Hersz

Eckstein – were Jews who had fled from Poland to Belgium. Following the German occupation, they had planned to travel to Spain by taking a train which could allow them to reach the Pyrenees. However, they had to stop in Perpignan due to Eckstein's mother's advanced stage of pregnancy. As his parents feared they would be deported if they went to Perpignan's hospital, they asked Eidenbenz if she would accept Eckstein's mother in Elne's maternity home. In the meantime, Eckstein's father hid in the barn of a house situated in the village of Thuir. As remembered by Eckstein, Eidenbenz did not just take care of his mother when she gave birth to him; she also protected them both when the Germans arrived in Thuir. Although Eidenbenz was expected to follow the Vichy government's laws, to avoid compromising the SRC's status as a neutral and independent organisation, she skirted round official orders. According to Eckstein, his case was not an exception, as Eidenbenz exchanged many Jewish children's names for Spanish ones when she registered their births. In so doing, Eidenbenz not only risked being dismissed from the Swiss Aid to Children organisation, but also being deported herself.

Nevertheless, Eidenbenz's humanitarian action fell into oblivion in the aftermath of the war. As Eckstein (2017) has pointed out, 'my parents returned to Belgium and tried to recontact the person who had helped them [Eidenbenz], but without success'. As an adult, Eckstein used to travel to the region of Perpignan each summer holidays with his family to learn more about the strange story of his birth, as well as about the woman who had directed Elne's maternity home. In 1991, he asked for a birth certificate at Elne's town hall and he then finally found her name. Eckstein obtained Eidenbenz's address via the SRC, which confirmed to him that she was still alive and resided in Rekawinkel on the outskirts of Vienna. Their encounter fifty years later shows to what extent experiences only become meaningful through the reception of memories, which radically transform our perception of what has happened. Rather than just being a happy coincidence, Eckstein and Eidenbenz's reunion allows us to comprehend that the process by which societies remember also has its own history.

In the same period that Eckstein found Eidenbenz, the Swiss historian Michèle Fleury-Seemuller met one of Eidenbenz's closest colleagues; the Swiss pediatric nurse Friedel Bohny-Reiter (1912–2001) who had also worked for the Swiss Aid to Children/SRC organisation assisting refugee children in Rivesaltes' camp. Like Eidenbenz, she hid many Jewish children in order to avoid that they were deported. Bohny-Reiter also kept a diary in which she recorded her experiences, including the first deportations which took place in Rivesaltes' camp. Seemuller convinced her to publish her testimony, which appeared in 1993. Another personality who also used to enjoy her summer holidays near Perpignan, the Swiss feminist filmmaker Jacqueline Veuve, eagerly read Bohny-Reiter's diary and decided to draw inspiration for her next cinematographic project from this personal account. Having already adapted Anne-Marie Im Hof-Piguet's *La Filière* (1985) for the screen – the testimony of another Swiss Aid to Children/SRC volunteer who secretly helped Jewish children to flee – Veuve became a key figure in the recollection of the memories of those female Swiss volunteers who had challenged the SRC's principles during the Second World War. Veuve's *Journal de Rivesaltes* was released in 1997. It was no coincidence that Eckstein attended the screening which was organised on the 2nd December of the same year in Perpignan in the presence of both Bohny-Reiter and Veuve.

As Brenda Lynn Edgar (2022, 103) has pointed out, the release of Veuve's film coincided with a critical moment of reassessment of both France's and Switzerland's involvement in the Second World War. In France, the trial of Maurice Papon – former secretary-general of the prefecture of Gironde – revealed the implication of the Vichy government in deportations, while in Switzerland the opening of the ICRC archives led the Swiss historian Jean-Claude Favez (1988) to conclude that this institution was aware of the exterminations perpetrated in Nazi camps. This strained context shows that Eckstein and Eidenbenz's encounter in 1991 should be inscribed within a broader movement aimed at raising collective awareness in both France and Switzerland of the implication of these countries in the Holocaust. Although female relief workers – such as Eidenbenz – had previously been completely ignored, they were rediscovered at the turn of the twenty-first century and became models of humanity thanks to the transmission of the fluctuating memories inherited by various communities. Ten years after she received a phone call from Eckstein, Eidenbenz was honoured by the Yad Vashem Institute as Righteous amongst the Nations – a year after her colleague Bohny-Reiter had received the same distinction. Besides the Jewish community, Eidenbenz's humanitarian action was praised by the Government of Catalonia in 2002 when she received the Creu de Sant Jordi. In turn, the Queen of Spain awarded Eidenbenz with the Cruz de Oro de la Orden Civil de la Seguridad Social in 2006 – a year before the Historical Memory Law was adopted in Spain. Also in 2007, the French ambassador to Austria bestowed her with the Légion d'honneur; a distinction which had paradoxically also been awarded to Papon in 1961 by the French Prime Minister Charles de Gaulle.

For Eckstein (2017) what is 'disturbing' is that both Eidenbenz and the perpetrators of crimes against humanity were said to have carried out their actions because of 'their sense of duty'. So, the question 'Does this mean that extreme evil and the most noble good are very close to each other?' still haunts

him. Eidenbenz – who became very close to Eckstein during the last twenty
years of her life – wrote a letter to him where she explained her motivations for
dedicating her life to helping those people who were in need:

> You asked me to explain my humanitarian engagement (...) If you see
> someone fall into water, a reflex means that you will try to save that person.
> It's my *Kategorische Imperativ* that compels me to help (...). Where my
> work in France is concerned (...) it was good for the refugees, but also for me
> personally. I was very happy and (...) felt that God had proposed this work to
> me. The work in Vienna was my own desire (...) And there, I received the gift
> of my life: Yetti's friendship. We have worked together for over sixty years
> and we still love each other (Eidenbenz 2008)

At the end of her life – when Eidenbenz was reliving her experiences with
Eckstein – she explained her humanitarian engagement by appealing to
Immanuel Kant's categorical imperative: the exceptionless universal moral
law which humans should follow by orienting themselves through their exclusively rational capacity to perform good will. Nevertheless, Adolf Eichmann –
the SS official in charge of the final solution – also declared during his trial in
1961 that 'he had lived his whole life according to Kant's moral precepts, and
especially according to a Kantian definition of duty'. As Arendt (2006b, 134–5) –
who was present at the trial – remarked 'there is no slightest doubt that in one
respect Eichmann did (...) follow Kant's precepts: a law is a law, there could be
no exceptions'. Unlike Eichmann, Eidenbenz preferred to resist governmental
decisions which would have made her an agent of injustice, what we call today
civil disobedience. Furthermore, Eindenbenz's choice revealed the limitations of
the SRC's humanitarian principles – such as neutrality and independence – for
helping the victims of crimes against humanity. The sharp dissonance between
these principles and her moral values inevitably led her to face ethical conflicts,
such as the occasion when the Gestapo visited Elne's maternity home to arrest
a young Jewish woman called Lucie. Eckstein has explained to me on several
occasions how guilty Eidenbenz felt for the rest of her life that she had not been
able to prevent Lucie's deportation.

   Although Eidenbenz said she acted in strict compliance with Kant's categorical imperative, she described in her letter that her work was a source of great
happiness; an affective state which Kant would not have accepted for justifying
an action in the domain of ethics. Rather than regarding morals as being just
a matter of rational thinking, she explained her humanitarian mission in France
as being in close connection with her religious sentiments. As remembered by
Eidenbenz, she felt that her humanitarian duty to refugees was a call from God;
a kind of spiritual revelation which shows the strong influence of Protestantism
in her life, as the daughter of the evangelist pastor Johann Albrecht Eidenbenz.

What Eidenbenz does not mention in her letter is that she tried to continue working for the SRC in the aftermath of the war, but her application was formally refused because she lacked the necessary experience. For Eckstein, there are two hypotheses which could explain the SRC's decision: either its members became aware of Eidenbenz's insubordination to the organisation's principles or of her sexual orientation.

Despite her rejection from the SRC, Eidenbenz was grateful as she received the best reward of her life in Austria: meeting Yetti, as her fellow humanitarian activist, and the love of her life, Henriette Hierhammer was also known. Together they funded the 'Schweizer Haus' in Vienna – a centre destined for welcoming refugee children under the auspices of the *Hilfswerk der Evangelischen Kirchen der Schweiz* (Relief Organisation of the Protestant Churches of Switzerland). Eckstein – who stayed at their house in Rekawinkel on numerous occasions – has told me that they lived their relationship openly. Although we can imagine that her experience as a sexual minority could have played an important role in her humanitarian engagement, Eckstein has assured me that she never made a reference to her sexual orientation when explaining her humanitarian work. In spite of this, contemporary scholars (Cassel et al. 2018) have interpreted her engagement as an expression of the – 'resistance of the LGBT community against fascism' showing that today Eidenbenz's experiences have become a model of queer humanitarianism. Instead, Eidenbenz insisted on describing her desire to help others as an automatic reflex. One can only wonder why she felt that doing good was the most natural reaction in a time when Western civilisation was revealing its darkest side. From a performative approach, Eidenbenz's humanitarian engagement can be interpreted as a perfect expression of the Swiss emotional habitus according to which she had learnt to feel attached to her country. By genuinely re-enacting Helvetic emotions such as compassion, Eidenbenz was showing that she had perfectly appropriated the scripted national orthodoxy, even if this was radically subversive for the SRC during the Second World War.

4 The French Touch

As Starobinski (1993, 21) explained, the very 'sense of the word civilisation' found 'in Hitlerism a barbarity unquestionably hideous enough to embody its opposite'. Reinventing the fragile experience of what being a human felt like in the aftermath of war started with the arduous humanitarian task of Europe's reconstruction. Acknowledging the lack of legal framework to ensure the protection of civilians in wartime, the ICRC adopted a new convention in 1949. Two years later, the newly created United Nations organisation approved the refugee convention, which redefined the right of displaced persons to flee their home countries because of their 'well-founded fear of being persecuted for reasons of race, religion, nationality, membership of a particular social group or political opinion'.[11] The creation of the category of refugee revealed that a spectre was 'haunting humanity' during the Cold War: 'the spectre of fear' (Bourke 2005, 14) provoked by the scenario of a future and *hotter* nuclear war, the thermic sensation with which international powers would start to measure the danger of a conflict.

The decolonisation process also marked a turning point in the negotiation of post-war emotional legacies, as it equated the pain of Jews during Second World War with that inflicted by Western powers in their colonies. These affective transfers allowed French intellectuals such as Jean-Paul Sartre (1968), to denounce the Vietnam War (1955–1975) as genocide, as well as the crimes committed by the French government during the Algerian War (1954–1962). The traumatic memories of the Holocaust were a key element in making Third-Worldism a revolutionary ideology which placed the hopes of humanity in those countries which were neither aligned with the United States nor with the Soviet Union's axis. Also moved by a renewed hope of liberating humanity from any form of oppression, students started their own revolution on the streets of Paris in May 1968. By raising their voices under slogans such as '*Nous sommes tous des Juifs allemands*' [We are all German Jews], the radical Left protested against Charles de Gaulle's decision to remove the resident permit of the leader of this movement: Daniel Cohn-Bendit, a Franco-German sociology student at Nanterre University, who was of Jewish descent.

As Eleanor Davy (2015, 40–1) has pointed out, the process through which Third-Worldism was created reached a milestone when a group of physicians who were sympathetic to the ideals of May 68 broke their initial affiliation with the ICRC during the Nigerian Civil War (1967–1970). To condemn the massacre perpetrated against the Biafran people by the Nigerian government, French doctors such as Kouchner – whose grandparents had died in the Auschwitz concentration camp – did not hesitate to decry this situation as genocide. According to 'the founding myth' (Desgrandchamps 2011), this group of physicians refused to act in compliance with 'the culture of silence' imposed by the ICRC because it was the same approach that this organisation had adopted concerning the existence of Nazi camps during Second World War (Brauman 2012, 1525). In 1971, some of these rebel humanitarians created – in collaboration with journalists – MSF: an organisation specifically oriented towards medical care, which renewed the humanitarian dream of alleviating human suffering by speaking out in the name of those populations

---

[11] See the convention approved by the United Nations High Commissioner for Refugees in 1951 here: www.unhcr.org/4ca34be29.pdf

who were in danger outside of the Western world. Despite its initial revolutionary ambitions, the members who are officially mentioned by MSF as its founders are all men.[12] More than a hundred years after Dunant's rallying cry, one could still wonder where the women within the humanitarian movement were. As this section suggests, graphic novels constitute exceptional materials for making women visible within MSF's history.

4.1 Human after All

Biafra – MSF's mythical founding moment – became a 'new Solferino' (Rufin 1986, 61) because the media managed to turn this conflict, as well as the related famine, into a highly emotional context which is frequently – and vaguely – referred to as a 'humanitarian crisis' (Desgrandchamps 2018, 87–8; Martín-Moruno 2022, 2). A former British colony, Nigeria became an independent country in 1960 containing a heterogeneous ethnic population including the Muslim Hausa of Northern Nigeria, the Muslim and Christians Yorubas of its south-western part and the Igbo Christians and animists of the south. In 1967, the military governor Odumegwu Emeka Ojukwu proclaimed the creation of the Republic of Biafra on the grounds of the massacres perpetrated by the Nigerian government against the Igbo population. Surrounded by the Nigerian army during two and half years, the Biafran population suffered from army attacks, forced displacement and epidemics, but most of all from a famine which became the first one to be broadcasted on television (Gorin 2013, 176).

A few months before May 68, the French public discovered other types of shocking images: that of starving Igbo children which were widely circulated as visual proof that Nigeria's blockade had been thoroughly planned to murder the Biafran population. Journalists did not hesitate to associate the situation in Biafra with genocide to conjure the ghostly presence of the Holocaust through its identification with the consequences of the West's Imperial past. The genocide became, thus, a sort of 'communication slogan' (Brauman 2000, 616) which was consciously used by those physicians who joined the mission organised by the ICRC in collaboration with the French Red Cross. Breaking with the ICRC's principle of confidentiality – which in these French Doctors' eyes aligned this organisation with the perpetrators of atrocities – their affective strategy was to make audiences feel guilty for collaborating in denying the existence of genocide. Rather than having its origins in compassion, the emotional roots of *témoignage* (speaking out) emerged from a collective sense of shame and indignation about the monster that humanity – as well as the so-called civilised world – incarnated after the Second World War.

---

[12] See MSF's website www.msf-me.org/about-us/history/founding-msf

But who actually were the French Doctors? At the head of this mission were two experienced physicians who had already worked for the ICRC during the Yemeni Civil War (1962–1970): Maximilien Récamier and Jean-Pascal Grellety-Bosviel. In a graphic novel, in which Grellety-Bosviel describes his fifty years of lived experiences as a humanitarian by combining his drawings, confessions and letters, I found a photograph of the French doctors who worked at the Awo-Omamma Hospital. The image's legend reads: 'In Biafra, Elisabeth and Minor Hernandez, Bernard Kouchner and Pascal Grelletty, at 3am after a night of surgical operations' (Grellety-Bosviel 2013, 54). Kouchner, who had not yet finished his medical studies, was one of the first volunteers to be recruited, alongside Récamier and Grellety-Bosviel. He left for Biafra in early September. Hernandez arrived some days later. He was a former Guatemalan doctor who worked at Lariboisière Hospital in Paris. However, I was not able to identify any historical records concerning the woman who also appeared in a doctor's uniform and who was identified as Hernandez's wife. Surprisingly, in the Spanish edition of Grellety-Bosviel's book this same image was present but with the surnames of these French Doctors written in red. Here the woman I was looking for was renamed Marot.[13]

Marot did not just have a surname; she also had a first name: Christiane. I learnt this from a friend of Kouchner: Patrick Valas who had also volunteered during the mission in Biafra as an anaesthetist and who defended his thesis on the Red Cross' medical team in Biafra on his return to Paris. Amongst the names he mentions in his thesis, there is 'Doctor Christiane Marrot' (Valas 1969, 10 and 27) who was a surgeon and part of the team supervised by Récamier in Awo-Omamma. In this hospital, French doctors primarily performed war surgery on wounded Biafran soldiers, albeit the lack of medical facilities frequently forced them to triage those who they would not be able to save from death. Besides the wounded, the face of suffering was represented by children with 'haggard eyes, swollen eyelids, white silky hair, the emaciated look of the thorax and upper members in contrast to the rest of their body which was swollen with fluid' who were treated in the former school of Santa-Anna (Valas 1969, 43). However, it was much harder to see the camps where persons suffering from cachexia died. As Valas (1969, 61) concludes, he had written his thesis:

> to bear witness to genocide, as amongst all of the explanations that have been given about the origins and evolution of this disaster, one fact remains (. . .) everything was put into place to exterminate a people: by means of a complete economic blockade supported by the bombing of civilian targets which has already killed 2 million people in 20 months.

---

[13] See the photograph on page 80 of the following link: www.editorialconfluencias.com/wp-content/pdf-paginas/PASCAL-Grellety-[71-93].pdf

Looking for more information about Marot, I contacted the ICRC archivist once again. Although I had previously received negative answers from him, he was happy to provide me with better news on this occasion. Marot had actually worked for the ICRC, but – as he told me – her mission only covered a brief period from the 19th September to the 30th November 1968. However, I could not access her dossier, as it was not yet open to the public. Without success, I also tried to obtain more information from Xavier Emmanuelli – cofounder of MSF – who was very close to Hernandez but who did not know the name of his partner during the Biafra mission. Although I was tempted to consider my research on Marot as a total failure, the fact that I had not been able to find more information about her also reveals that gender equality was not a priority on the French doctors' agenda. Even though students had proclaimed a sexual revolution during May 68, leadership was still associated with men in the public sphere. Within the humanitarian field, this masculinist vision appears to be represented in *The French Doctors*; a book written by the French journalist Olivier Weber who also dedicated some words to Marot.

> The doctors of Awo Omamma are holding up well. Two women contribute, through their presence, to boosting the morale of the troops: Christiane Marot, twenty-seven years old, surgeon and partner of Minor Hernandez, by whom she is pregnant, and Anne-Marie Barbé, general practitioner who works in the Santana dispensary, ten kilometres from the hospital. They comment on the daily news thanks to the copy of *Le Monde* that they receive from the Red Cross plane, sometimes as early as the day after it has been printed. They take the wounded to bathe in the river, where men wade about with plaster casts up to their throats. They bring a touch of gaiety to this end-of-the-world universe (Weber 1995, 58)

From my partial perspective, what sounds extremely shocking to me when I read these words is that these two female physicians are represented as being in charge of 'boosting the morale of the troops'. This was a military expression frequently used to refer to the mission of Red Cross nurses who were seen to take care of soldiers through tender feelings in order to encourage the masculinity of those fighting in warfare. In Weber's account about the origins of the French Doctors, women were still considered as secondary agents who were in Biafra not because of their ideals or medical skills, but instead to instil some comfort in this male universe. Although Marot appears in a photograph with her male colleagues after performing surgery, Weber's reference to her as Hernandez's partner with whom she was presumably expecting a baby shows the long-lasting and pernicious effects of patriarchy within the humanitarian movement. Besides Weber's description, the absence of information about the only female surgeon – whom I have been able to identify – who joined the

ICRC's mission in Biafra is material proof of the violence that can be exerted through the silences of history.

4.2 Cold War

Grellety-Bosviel was not an exceptional case within MSF, as French doctors and journalists belonging to this organisation have developed a particular taste for shaping the meaning of their humanitarian experiences through graphic novels. As Juliette Fournot (quoted in Martinez 2013) – who gradually became logistics coordinator, director and head of MSF's medical mission in Afghanistan throughout the 1980s – declared 'we have a duty to bear witness, even if we go there for health-care'. 'This force of testimony exists thanks to graphic novels', such as *The Photographer*. This three-volume work puts into dialogue the black and white photographs taken by the French photojournalist Didier Lefèvre – during his three-month mission in Afghanistan – with the drawings, captions and word balloons drawn by the cartoonist Emmanuel Guibert and the scenarios designed by graphic artist Frédéric Lemercier. This powerful textual and visual combination shows – in all its cruel nudity – what the Cold war meant: a euphemism used by the major world powers to refer to a long period of armed peace, which was achieved by fighting proxy wars in the emotionally distant Third World. This was the case of the Soviet-Afghan War (1979–1989) which confronted Kabul's Communist regime, which was supported by the Soviet Union's army, against insurgent Muslim militias such as the Mujahedeen who were backed – amongst others – by the United States, United Kingdom and Pakistan. The invasion of the Red Army resulted not only in the brutal killing of around one and a half million Afghans, but also in the displacement of 'the third of the population' of this country which fled towards Pakistan and Iran because of the repression of Kabul's Communist regime (Monsutti 2005, xiii).

Fournot – who is portrayed on the cover of the second volume of *The Photographer* – was not only one of the protagonists of this comic; she also played an important role in inspiring its plot. This was due to her documentary *A Ciel Ouvert* [Under an Open Sky] which recorded the MSF's 1986 operation which crossed one thousand kilometres of arid, mountainous terrain to transport medical supplies from Pakistan to Afghanistan. As Fournot explained to me during an interview, she proposed that Lefèvre should join the team to document the work that MSF was conducting in Afghanistan. Like Fournot's documentary, Lefèvre's four thousand photographs were intended to faithfully capture MSF's experiences with a twofold purpose: to inform MSF, as well as to testify to Afghan suffering due to a war which attracted little media interest at the time.

In *The Photographer*, bearing witness is particularly associated with the scene in which Fournot – who is referred to by her Afghan nickname – appears represented with her camera, filming a three-year-old child victim of the Soviet Air force's bombardment of Pütstük, while she says through tears to Lefèvre: 'the mother said to me, "Film it, Jamila. People have to know"' (Guibert et al. 2008, 140). Far from the heroic image symbolised by the French Doctors' notion of *témoignage* in Biafra, speaking out is presented in *The Photographer* as a moral duty which is performed with the feelings of impotence, suffering and sadness that were shared by the members of this mission before the slaughter of Afghans.

Rather than exploring the emotional universe of the MSF team, Fournot's film focuses on recording the difficult material conditions under which it became possible to provide medical care to Afghan people. In this sort of ethnographic document, her gaze visually positions Afghans as the real protagonist of the documentary to humanise the people who were dying not only due to bomb attacks, but also because they lacked any type of medical assistance. Although one of MSF's major concerns was bearing witness, Fournot planned this operation in total secrecy in order to ensure the security of her team, as MSF was not authorised to operate in Afghanistan and, therefore, the team had to work clandestinely.[14] As Fournot (quoted in Agence France-Presse 2021) has clarified, 'we were affiliated to political parties to guarantee our protection'. This means that 'we were not neutral', but we tried to 'remain impartial' by providing medical aid without any distinction. 'The logistic were an absolute headache' – added Fournot. MSF's team needed to transport medical supplies from Peshawar to the Northern valleys of Teschnkan and Yatfal in caravans towed by horses while wearing *chadris* – traditional female Muslim clothes which cover the body from head to foot – to avoid being identified at the border. Once in Afghanistan, French doctors changed their outfits for male Afghan clothes – including local caps such as *pakols*. Costumes allowed Fournot to act according to local expectations, by performing the fluidity of her gender identity, and overcome obstacles to introducing herself to her interlocutors as a reliable person. Fournot's ability to demonstrate her leadership in an exclusively masculine milieu was crucial for planning a safe passage to the MSF team's final destination. In *The Photographer,* Fournot explains – to Lefèvre – the secret of her negotiations as follows:

> At first, I surprised all of them with my knowledge of their language. And I'd generally take advantage of that surprise to assert myself. Plus, I know their traditions. You'll never see me reach out my hand to them, stare at them, or do anything that could humiliate them. And I try to speak calmy and with

---

[14] Prior to 1985, Pakistan also refused to allow MSF teams to work on its soil.

authority. There's a certain tone I use, which means, 'Okay, I'm a woman, but I'm the leader' (Guibert et al. 2008, 42)

As Lefevre remarks – through the photographer character – 'for an Afghan, a chief is a strong figure. There's no way a woman can be a chief. And yet they all understand that Juliette is the boss' (Guibert et al. 2008, 41). Fournot – who in 1986 was a thirty-two-year-old physician – managed to achieve this because she spoke Farsi fluently and knew exactly how to respect the cultural codes of this country. In the 1960s, her parents – Jacques and Madeleine Fournot – moved to Afghanistan with her and taught her their love for local traditions. Fournot's father, who was an engineer who worked for the United Nations Development Program, became a highly respected personality amongst Afghans. What Fournot learnt from him was that to aid Afghan people it was necessary to involve them in this process to create a community that worked on mutual trust. Fournot succeeded in leading a humanitarian operation in an extremely dangerous war context, marked by risks and constant uncertainty, because she built trust within a network of local people who actively collaborated with the MSF team. As an 'affective state and attitude', trust enables the creation of an emotional bond through 'horizontal relations, rather than vertical and hierarchical ones' (Frevert 2013, 1 and 39). Beyond compassion – 'a moral sentiment with no possible reciprocity' (Fassin 2012, 3) – Fournot was perceived as someone who could be trusted, because she built a relationship with Afghans that was based on values such as respect rather than authority. This community building approach – which has become a trending topic in current debates about the necessity of decolonising humanitarian aid – remains the condition for avoiding the transformation of humanitarian care into a form of domination. By adopting this perspective, Fournot's team was not only able to save the lives of many wounded people by performing surgery with only basic materials, but also to provide gynaecological and paediatric care, as the presence of female healthcare staff inspired confidence amongst Afghan women.

While trust became the key that allowed the MSF team to access Afghan hearts, the Soviet government revealed increasing distrust of Fournot who was accused – by Kabul's media – of being a drug trafficker during her youth. Trust and distrust were not only central emotions used by superpowers to control the nuclear arms race during the Cold War; they also regulated the local interactions of the MSF team in Afghanistan. For instance, Fournot still considers today that distrustful Soviet accusations against her were the sign that her team was doing good work. Challenging MSF's image as a group of white male saviours, Fournot became a unique leader within this organisation because of the personal qualities that she embodied for her team as well as Afghan people. She did this by maintaining trust;

'an affective bond which requires permanent dedication and involvement' (Klimke et al. 2016, 4) otherwise, trust can be destroyed, like when a friend is betrayed. Although Fournot left this country in 1989, her mission really finished in 2011, when she was invited to present her film in Moscow. As she told me, this occasion enabled her to fulfil the promise she had made to that mother in Pütstük: that she would film the corps of her child to show audiences the atrocities committed by the Red Army. By screening these images in front of former Russian combatants and civil rights activists, Fournot was returning the gift that the Afghans had offered her: their trust, the most perfect expression of friendship. Although the Soviet-Afghan war is associated with the end of the Cold War, because it led to the collapse of the Soviet Union, Afghans are still suffering from the consequences of the artificial frontiers that were traced by Imperial powers during the decolonisation process. 'These are the wounds which continue to bleed' commented Fournot (2022) in a podcast, in which she returns to her experiences of more than forty years previously.

5 Blue Humanitarianism

Humanity has historically evolved as an essentially political concept, and the same can be said for the notion of nature, as it has been claimed by those persons who consider themselves as humans to distinguish themselves from those others who only look like animals. Although the Enlightenment concept of civilisation shaped our humanness by opposition to a primitive state of nature – which mankind was expected to domesticate through the progress of science and technology – the invention of the atomic bomb paradoxically alerted us to the risks of disentangling human and environmental morality. Living in the era of the Anthropocene, it has become impossible to think about our humanness without reframing it in close interconnection with non-human agents such as the Earth, the rocks, the trees and the oceans. By adhering to the oceanic cultural turn in the humanities, a field now referred to as 'Blue Humanities' – a fluid area of research bringing together environmental studies and maritime history, as well as science and literary studies (Alaimo 2019) – this section explores a distinctive way of knowing, feeling and performing humanitarianism which has historically evolved in relation to the conception of the Mediterranean as 'a system in which nature and humankind reconcile' (Braudel 1999, 7).

By focusing on the study of the rescue missions led by the German captain, biologist, human and animal rights activist Pia Klemp, I suggest considering this specific form of aid as an expression of – what I call here – blue humanitarianism. This is not merely because its main backdrop is the sea, moreover, and most importantly, Klemp's activism exemplifies an environmentally oriented form of care, which suggests reframing the notion of vulnerability within an ecological perspective that embraces the sea's material and phenomenological distinctiveness. Klemp's operations in the Mediterranean cannot be fully understood without taking into consideration her militancy in initiatives aimed at the protection and conservation of oceans and marine wildlife within organisations such as Sea Shepherd. This approach to care becomes manifest in her book *Lass uns mit den Toten tanzen* [Let us dance with the dead], where she describes her mission as captain of the Louise Michel – the vessel founded by the artist Banksy in 2020 – 'a boat full of revolt and devotion, led by a small antifascist, anarchofeminist, vegan' and 'intersectional collective' (Klemp 2021, 12). An analysis of this autobiographical account, as well as of Klemp's discourses, will allows us to interpret her experiences as an emotional immersion in the waters of sadness, love, shame and indignation. Her blue humanitarianism compels us to think about the ways through which the notion of humanity is evolving through a new generation of humanitarian activists.

5.1 Caring for the Mediterranean

In *Let us dance with the dead*, Klemp shares her experiences as the captain of search and rescue ships such as the *Iuventa* and the *Sea-Watch 3*: vessels which have operated in the Mediterranean since 2016 in order to save people travelling on unsafe boats from drowning. Klemp's book has only been translated into French through the provocative title *Les vivants, les morts et les marins* [The Living, the Dead and the Sailors]. This choice of translation makes an explicit reference to the famous quotation which states that 'there are three sorts of people: those who are alive, those who are dead, and those who are at sea', which was probably formulated by the philosopher Anacharsis in the early sixth century BCE (Philips 2020, 17). These words show the long-standing fascination that humans have cultivated for sailors because they are imagined to be a special race of beings who have acquired practical knowledge of the stars, the winds and the waters, as well as exceptional abilities for facing the unknown – which is symbolised by the sea. In fact, this quote summarises the specific experience of seafaring: neither being alive nor dead, but instead feeling like a sort of Odysseus whose life is hanging in suspense before them.

Far from mythical representations, for Klemp being a twenty-first century sailor means looking like the members of her crew: citizen activists who have joined organisations such as *Jugend Rettet* or *Sea-Watch*. In her narrative, she refers to them as an exclusive club, which has selected its VIP members for their abilities to preserve the duty of providing assistance to any person found in danger at sea. Klemp (2021, 24) describes her crew as being composed of people who do not have 'any true experience of the sea'. They have just done 'a bit of sailing at the week-end' and display a certain amount of 'sympathy for pirates', as well as 'a more or less authentic interest in weather-related phenomena'. In Klemp's words (2021, 27) they are 'a bunch of hippies, punks, righters of wrongs and fighters with weird tattoos and hairstyles'. As characterized by Klemp (2021, 30) just a 'few of them have a normal life where they have to make apologies in order to join us in the search and rescue zone'. As Klemp (2021, 30) concludes, these people are 'a sample of the very best of humanity'.

Although maritime stories have been presented as a male domain – probably because the sea is considered to be too dangerous for ladies – figures such as Klemp, as well her colleague, the German ship captain and climate change activist Carola Rackete (1988–), remind us that women can also embark on sea operations, thus, defying gender expectations about what a sailor should look like. In fact, Klemp and Rackete are not just a rare exception, as their stories are inscribed in a long tradition of female mariners who have joined scientific expeditions since the Enlightenment period. For instance, the French botanist Jeanne Baret (1740–1807) circumnavigated the world as an assistant to Louis-Antoine de Boungainville's natural expedition in the late eighteenth century. Similarly, Rose de Freycinet (1794–1832) navigated around the globe with her husband, the French navy officer Louis de Freycinet, who was in charge of the scientific expedition aboard the *Uranie*. Also the Spanish nurse Isabel Zendal y Gómez participated in – what has been referred to as – 'the first humanitarian mission in the world' (Perigüell and Añón 2003, 8): the Royal Philanthropic Vaccine Expedition commissioned by Dr Francisco Javier Balmis, under the auspices of Charles IV's Empire, to introduce Jenner's smallpox vaccine to Spanish America and Asia aboard the *María Pita*. Neither should we forget that maritime stories have also been a central episode in missions led by women, such as Nightingale who arrived with her corps of nurses in the Crimea aboard the *Vectis*. Others, such as Kea crossed the Atlantic to help Spanish Republicans by travelling aboard a ship named *Paris*.

Despite their disparate geographical and temporal locations, all of these women's stories share a characteristic: the blueness of the sea which, thus, emerges as 'a space in which we can theorise the materiality' of their journeys (Oppermann 2019, 447). Amongst them, Klemp's *The Living, the Dead and the Sailors* represents an exceptional narrative for rethinking the meaning of care in the framework of blue humanitarianism. This is a form of humanitarianism which challenges traditional perceptions that humanitarian action is mainly 'territorial' and 'located on the ground' or 'in the field'. As Imogen Dobbie has recently pointed out, scholars need to 'make the maritime visible' within humanitarian history in order to better understand specific forms of aid which have gone well beyond providing food and medical care and focus on 'the most basic act of saving life by pulling it out of the waves' (Dobbie 2020). Moving this line of research further, I understand Klemp's activism as a post-humanist form of care which is rooted in a 'seascape epistemology' (Ingersoll 2016, 6) that allows her to navigate through the interactions that operate between humans and non-humans – including 'things', 'other animals', 'physical' and 'spiritual forces' – in the climate regime of the Anthropocene (de la Bellacasa 2017, 1).

In her autobiographical account, Klemp introduces herself as a sailor who is waiting for her next mission in the New Lion Bar – a pub close to the Port of Valletta in Malta – while she drinks some beers with her quartermaster Jeremy. They are the only two white persons there and Klemp (2021, 16) is the sole woman, as the New Lion Bar is a meeting point for 'travelers to lost destinations'. Through a long interior monologue, Klemp explains to what extent her life makes no sense on land: 'the periods on the quayside are always crap, and I suddenly feel in a really bad mood'. 'It's time to set sail', because we 'cannot leave them alone over there, whether they are human beings or not'. However, to do this she needs her ship which she characterises as having full agency, including the ability to express and feel emotions. Her vessel is not 'a classical beauty', as 'rusty streaks are spilling over her blue paint, like make-up blurred by tears'. It is as if the old blue tub – adds Klemp (2021, 21) – was singing the lyrics to Lesley Gore's hit 'It's my party and I will cry if I want to'.[15] The old blue ship – to which Klemp refers – is the *Iuventa* on which she commanded her first mission in the Central Mediterranean from August 2016 to August 2017. In Klemp's eyes (2021, 186) the *Iuventa* is crying, because she is mourning the Mediterranean: one of the deadliest frontiers in the world. The *Iuventa* crying – as used by Klemp in her narrative – functions as a blue metaphor for her emotional communion with her ship, as well as with the Mediterranean, as its seawaters are salty like human tears (Oppermann 2019, 446).

Although the EU is not officially at war, Klemp considers that its member countries have declared merciless warfare against those people who are labelled as irregular migrants, because they are considered as a threat to its security. On the twenty-first century *mare nostrum*, attacks against human rights are not perpetrated by a traditional army but rather by Frontex: the European border and coast guard agency, which organises forced deportations in close cooperation with Libya to resettle migrants in camps based in this country, where they can be subjected to human trafficking, rape and torture. Even if they are displaced persons fleeing poverty and violence, European countries resist granting them with the rights of refugees, showing the limits of this category which does not recognise trafficked

---

[15] Lesly Gore became a feminist icon in the 1960s when she released this song.

people, irregular immigrants or those at risk of deportation as persons of concern. Rather than referring to them as migrants or refugees, Klemp (2021, 22) prefers to call them their 'guests' aboard the *Iuventa* in order to stress that they are individuals who have the right to seek freedom in Europe and, therefore, also to have safe passage through the Mediterranean. Despite the efforts made on the *Iuventa* to take care of their guests, Klemp witnesses with desperation that they are treated 'like animals' on their arrival in Europe. 'How sad!' – exclaims Klemp (2021, 70) – 'as not even animals deserve to be treated like them'.

By looking at the pain embodied by the Mediterranean, Klemp transforms her initial blue feelings into a combat, which she understands more as a part of her antifascist fight, rather than as a result of her humanitarian commitment. Indeed, this is a central characteristic of many 'demotic humanitarians': citizen activists acting within grassroots initiatives who 'barely use the term humanitarian itself' in order to describe their rescue missions (Taithe 2019, 1782). Although the Red Cross and MSF have imposed a culture of humanitarianism which presents itself as apolitical, a wide range of partisan actors have played a fundamental role in humanitarian initiatives, thus blurring its frontiers with the human rights movement. For instance, 'the French *grande dame* of anarchy', Louise Michel – to whom Klemp (2021, 12) dedicates her book – was a key personality in the organisation of relief efforts during the Paris Commune through her involvement in the creation of a corps of ambulance women (Martín-Moruno 2019). This is the anarchist heritage that Klemp (2021, 106) claims in her narrative in order to summarise her engagement in the Mediterranean through the slogan 'Fuck charity – love solidarity.' By rephrasing the Uruguayan writer Fernando Galeano (2001, 312), we can differentiate 'solidarity, which is horizontal and takes place between equals' from charity, which 'is top-down' and, therefore, 'humiliating for those who receive it' because it never challenges 'the implicit power relations'.

Solidarity emerges, thus, as the driving force that allows the crew of the *Iuventa* to navigate through the Mediterranean towards 'the horizon' of a shared utopia, which – as Eduardo Galeano (1993) put it (quoted by Klemp 2021, 1) – they 'will never reach', but it serves to keep them sailing. This utopia is moved by the hope that another world can be possible: a blue planet where 'crew love' – which is Klemp's 'true love' – invites us to dance to the rhythms of the waves, the winds and the animals. Klemp's anarchist militancy turns the Mediterranean into a sort of spiritual agent with which she celebrates the baptism of the *Iuventa* in the sea of revolution.

> The sea opens up ahead of us (. . .) From now on, we are our own planet and we are floating, free from the theatre of society (. . .) The deep blue sea splashes the hull while the first puffins fly in acrobatic circles around us (. . .)

> The waves are now two metres high and the sea is unleashing itself more and more. The air is so pure that it even seeps into our smallest alveoli (...) I shift my body weight from one foot to the other and surf on my boat with the movement of the waves, imagining that I'm the one pushing it through the water with the strength of my muscles (Klemp 2021, 53)

Klemp's experience of the seawaters, the weather, the animals and, even, of her ship – which becomes an extension of her own body – illustrates perfectly well what blue humanitarianism represents: that is a form of aiding people in distress at sea, in which humans appear as just one part of a broader system regulated by the interactions between the physical, biological and technological environment. Within this blue humanitarianism, organising care involves understanding and feeling oneself to be in intimate connection with currents, waves, winds, sea life and, above all, ships. Indeed, the crew of the *Iuventa* need to negotiate the localisation of people in distress with these agents, taking onboard as many persons as possible. Beyond the practical conditions that are necessary for search and rescue operations, care also involves performing the revolutionary values shared by the crew of the *Iuventa*: solidarity and resistance (Klemp 2021, 13). In a TEDx speech given in Berlin, Klemp delves into the emotional depths of her engagement in the Mediterranean, providing us with some clues for better understanding what she defines as solidarity.

> I am part of a generation that grew up asking their grand-parents 'what did you do against it?' And I come to realise that I am also a part of a generation that will have to answer the very same question to our grandchildren (Klemp 2019)

In so saying, Klemp (2019) is establishing a direct connection between the Holocaust and – what she identifies as the objective of the European political project – 'the transformation of the Mediterranean into a mass grave for migrants'. Even if she is not specifically using the term genocide, Klemp is inscribing herself within humanitarian history's long tradition of denouncing crimes against humanity that result from the lack of an orchestrated political response from international powers. In so doing, Klemp is mobilising a painful emotion in front of her audience in Berlin: shame. Shame that arises from the consciousness of the guilt that Germans have negotiated as a nation in order to come to terms with their Nazi past (Frevert 2020, 203). Also fighting against the culture of silence around the deaths of people in the Mediterranean – which is intended to dissimulate the responsibility of the EU in this tragedy – Klemp performs a self-righteous form of anger through her words: indignation.[16] As Barbara Rosenwein (2020, 227) has

---

[16] In her book *Wutschrift* (2022), Klemp frequently describes her anger by using the German term *Empörung*, which means indignation. To go further on the plural ancestry of anger in contemporary society, see Dixon (2020).

pointed out, in late–eighteenth century moral philosophy this particular form of anger was reserved for those people 'whose anger was dignified' and, therefore 'honorable'. In the twenty-first century, indignation has evolved as a political emotion linked to social justice through protest movements which have connected the shores of the Mediterranean, including the Arab Spring and the Spanish Indignados (Solera 2017, 7). Echoing this culture of indignation, Klemp seeks to raise awareness about our duty as citizens to fight for the dignity of those people who – even if they are regarded as rightless – should also be members of our humanity.

In her TEDx talk, Klemp (2019) makes a public call for solidarity, which for her means 'nothing that can be thought', as it has 'to be done'. In the name of solidarity, she says 'I do not need to make foreign problems, worries or oppression my own', instead I just have to recognise 'that all these problems are my very own from the beginning'. In many ways Klemp's notion of solidarity resembles the definition which Hannah Arendt (2006a, 265–8) pro-posed in her seminal work *On Revolution*, as it implies the necessity of a world which mediates the concern of those who suffer and the people who decide to remove or, at least, ameliorate this suffering. 'Though it may be aroused by suffering', solidarity 'is not guided by it', as it remains the principle which reminds us that someone else is suffering and not ourselves. In the light of Arendt's reflections, Klemp's notion of solidarity appears, therefore, as the prerequisite for avoiding the emotional identification which is promised by empathy, as well as for channelling emotions such as indignation into a collective action aimed at caring for those people who risk their lives in the Mediterranean. Klemp's vision of solidarity does not only challenge gender expectations, it also challenges the EU's anti-migrant policies which have led to her crew facing a jail sentence.

5.2 Guilty Solidarities

Although Klemp asserts her leadership with resolution amongst the members of her crew, her role as a captain frequently reveals the existence of gender troubles in the Mediterranean. Amongst the many examples of sexism that Klemp dissects in her narrative, she reproduces a conversation with the Libyan Coast Guard Navy over satellite phone, which is particularly representative of how care can become a subversive form of power for fighting against Patriarchy in the Mediterranean. ' – I want to speak to the captain' – says a male voice in awkward English and Klemp (2021, 68) answers: 'this is the captain speaking, sir'. Shocked at hearing a young female voice, the Libyan Coast Guard replies: 'Ah, my lady captain! (...) You stop taking migrants! Migrants go to Libya!'

Once again, Klemp's interior monologue gives us more details about her reaction to the paternalistic attitude displayed by the Libyan Coast Guard: 'My Lady Captain? Does he think we're in a medieval-themed film?' Hardening his tone, the Libyan Coast Guard addresses Klemp with aggressiveness: ' – You bring migrants here! (. . .) This is an order'. However, Klemp replies with assertiveness: 'Sir, according to international law and the Law of the Sea I would commit a crime if I did that.' To put an end to the conversation, she adds 'please, don't call this number again'.

By welcoming their guests aboard the *Iuventa*, Klemp is aware that she is not only defying gender expectations in the Mediterranean, but also that she and her crew are putting their own lives at risk. Solidarity is not just an act of resistance; it is an attitude which is being criminalised in the Mediterranean. In the end, the *Iuventa* was seized by Italian authorities after they accused several members of the mission of having cooperated with human traffickers in order to facilitate illegal immigrants' journeys. The crew of the *Iuventa*, which is still awaiting trial, could face twenty years in prison for these charges. Klemp (2021, 117) describes the end of the *Iuventa*'s mission as a tearing moment, when she had to separate herself from her ship, which – in turn – 'sends us a last goodbye' through her 'soft and sad navigation lights'. On leaving the *Iuventa*, she explains how her 'crew love' turned into 'crew blues' (Klemp 2021, 193): a blue mood which reflects to what extent she felt the loss of her ship as the amputation of a limb from her own body.

For Klemp, 'it is as arbitrary as it is presumptuous to draw a line between us and animals lying dead in fridges (. . .) as well as between us and the anonymous refugees floating in the sea' (Klemp 2021, 138). For her, being committed to solidarity means struggling against the root causes of both racism and climate change, which are indeed the result of the same phenomenon: the merciless exploitation propelled by the Capitalist system. Empathy will not save humanity from the ongoing refugee crisis nor from climate change, as this emotion only serves to justify – but not to remove – the hierarchies of powers which are at the roots of the neoliberal economic order (Pedwell 2014, 14). These are the hierarchies which establish a distinction between humans and non-humans – whether they are animals or just persons – who are losing their lives day after day, as they seek to reach the EU.

Klemp's story shows us to what extent the painful resonances of the Second World War – namely those linked to the Holocaust – still remain to be lived in the Western world as a turning point for mirroring the suffering of humanity and evidencing its higher degree of morality. 'To aid in the project of decolonising history', future historians of emotions and the senses should establish a larger framework for 'diversifying and complicating current accounts of human experience that remain western-centric conscious' (Barclay 2021, 465). Decolonising emotions is also crucial if historians want to concentrate on those humans 'who were at the receiving end' (Frevert 2016, 56).

6 Moral Economies of Care

Although the Red Cross movement adopted Nightingale's representation as the lady with the lamp as the official model according to which future generations of female volunteers would be affectively trained, compassion did not reflect the complexity nor the scale of the obstacles and conflictual experiences that these women would actually encounter in the field of operations. For instance, the security guidelines written in the 1990s by the British Red Cross nurse Claire Bertschinger (1953–) – who was awarded the Florence Nightingale medal – that she entitled '*What they don't tell you in Geneva*' show the tensions between individuals and organisations. Also, the more local cultures of humanitarian aid illustrated by Kea and Eidenbenz have allowed us to recognise the extent to which their experiences have been reified as models of black and queer activism, respectively, even though they did not define their engagement in the light of their racial or sexual identities. While Marot remains the speechless emissary of the French doctors in Biafra, Fournot openly refuses her heroic characterisation as the blond MSF girl who ventured into Afghanistan in the 1980s. Despite the current young generation of activists – such as Klemp – mocking gender expectations about what female captains should look like, they are frequently caricaturised by the media as tattooed pirates. Symbolising a cultural deviation from the image of the nurturing woman which has been cultivated within the humanitarian movement, the stereotypical representations of female relief agents today still reveal a dark obsession with the control of women's sexualities. Even worse, these clichés have contributed to marginalising the legitimate knowledge which these women have produced together – although not always in harmonious relation – with their male colleagues and the beneficiaries of their aid from the Crimean War onwards. But, how should we epistemologically approach women humanitarians' experiences in order to interpret them as the empirical basis of a valuable knowledge which goes well beyond medicine and its allied sciences and that can potentially inform us about the global challenges ahead – including gender equality?

To answer this question, I suggest exploring the potentialities of – what I call – moral economies of care: ways of knowing, feeling and performing humanitarianism which have emerged in close interaction with shifting ideals about who is worthy of receiving aid, as well as with related feelings which have informed the ways through which care should be provided to its recipients. My definition clearly differs from the notion of moral economies proposed by Didier Fassin (2009, 42) as a 'new configuration' which 'assigns a special place to moral sentiments in the public sphere' and which explained the emergence of a politics of compassion in the 1990s as the expansion of a global humanitarian governance. Nor is my use of this concept inspired by the meaning which Edward P. Thompson (1971, 76) gave it: 'a consistent traditional view of social norms and obligations, of the proper economic function of various parties within the community (...) which can be said to constitute the moral economy of the poor'. Instead, I am borrowing this category from the work conducted by historians of science, starting with Lorraine Daston (1995, 4) who defines a moral economy as a 'web of affect-saturated values that stand and function in well-defined relationship to one another', which guides the daily practices of a community of researchers on a normative level. Daston's moral economies have been particularly influential in emotion history, as shown by the proliferation of theses on this theme that have been produced under the auspices of the Centre for the History of Emotions based at the Max Planck Institute for Human Development in Berlin.[17] A recent publication edited by Ute Frevert (2019) summarises the plasticity of this category for exploring the complex historical relations that have been established between the economical and the moral universe. Putting more stress on the links between morals and science, rather than between morals and the market, Rob Boddice (2018, 223) has crafted a definition which is particularly useful for understanding how emotions are embedded in the 'patterns of thought that bolster everyday practices' and are – in their turn – 'formalised' 'into epistemologies that justify multilayered world-views'. This is not only valid for studying how scientists work in the laboratory, it can also be successfully applied to humanitarianism in order to comprehend care as a complex activity which implies both a moral and emotional dimension, as well as a set of caring practices which become – through their performance – specific ways of knowing, feeling and dealing with pain that are incarnated by a plethora of organisations and grassroots collectives.[18]

As shown by the stories gathered together in this Element, moral economies of care have gradually shed light on the suffering of different

---

[17] For more information about this doctoral program, see: www.mpib-berlin.mpg.de/research/research-centers/history-of-emotions/imprs-moral-economies

[18] Although some studies (Hass 1992; Taithe 2016) have shed light on the changing systems of knowledge, policies and practices that have emerged throughout humanitarian history, they have not yet integrated emotions as a central epistemic element for understanding the evolution of the humanitarian ethos.

collectives: wounded and sick soldiers at the heart of Western Empires, victims of mass atrocities during the long Second World War, third world populations throughout the decolonisation process, as well as migrants and the Earth in the Anthropocene era. Rather than being examples of exceptional women, these case studies are representative of how moral economies of care have been created in particular contexts that have been marked by a specific target of violence. Reframing what it means to be human – through Imperialist, human-rights, South and blue seascape epistemologies – what we can learn from these stories is that our sense of humanity has been reshaped by disparate values such as charity, dignity, friendship and solidarity. Beyond the legal framework provided by humanitarian law and human rights, I understand moral economies of care as having been essentially forged by historically situated practices – the materiality of which enables us, furthermore, to analyse the gendered dynamics operating within organisations and grassroots initiatives.

By considering humanitarianism as a historical development of an ethics of care (Barnett 2011, 8), moral economies enable us not only to make women visible within this movement, but also to shed light on the power dynamics established under the wings of different cultures of humanitarian aid. Thus, this category opens the door to examining women's appropriation, negotiation and contestation of the values claimed by those male experts who have traditionally been at the head of humanitarian organisations. Zooming in and out, moral economies appear to be an extremely powerful category for detecting the resistances exerted by women against hegemonic gender, class and racial ideologies within humanitarian history, as well as for exploring how they challenged institutional views through the expression of subversive feelings such as contempt, resentment, hope, love, shame, trust and indignation. This *jeux d'échelle*s approach (Revel 1996) enables us to observe that moral economies are not fixed constructions; they are in continuous transformation because the practices mobilised by individual actors can come into conflict with the values prescribed by organisations and, thus, prompt their structures to change. By focusing on power dynamics, moral economies of care allow us to shed light on the interactions which regulate the affective exchanges between the institutional framework and individuals. Thus, moral economies of care appear to be a category which can enable the deconstruction of essentialist visions of femininity, as well as the representations of 'toxic masculinities' (Taithe 2020) which are present throughout the history of humanitarian relief: a domain which is yet to be fully explored itself.

Moreover, moral economies establish a fertile theoretical framework for historicising care not just as a moral concern that one can feel for somebody who is in distress: what Fisher and Tronto (1990, 40) refer to as 'caring about'. The malleability of this category of care also allows us to contextualise the material conditions under which it becomes possible to 'take care of' the situation in order 'to predict (. . .) the outcome of our action', as well as the necessary caring tasks that should be performed for satisfying a specific need i.e. 'care giving' (Fisher and Tronto 1990, 42–3). Last but not least, moral economies enable us to hear the voice of those groups which have received care and, thus, to examine the conflicts that have been experienced between both female and male relief agents and the recipients of their aid. Under the lenses of moral economies of care, we can, thus, navigate through the evolution of a multifarious humanitarian knowledge – 'coloured by sensations, feelings, memories and thoughts' (Martín-Moruno 2023b) – which has been produced across the disciplinary frontiers imposed by nursing, gynaecology, nutrition sciences, war surgery and oceanography and that has frequently involved a strong spiritual dimension whether it was openly inspired by religious feelings or more revolutionary hopes. Most importantly, moral economies of care give us the opportunity to restore the experiences of those female agents who have been frequently neglected in humanitarian history as a trustworthy knowledge. A trustworthy knowledge which they have constructed alongside their male colleagues, while lacking their authority.

I hope that my moral economies of care could be a useful category for future historians working at the crossroads of gender, emotions, experiences and humanitarianism and, in particular, for Marie Leyder. Looking back to the time that we have spent together discussing moral economies of care, I am only able to feel nostalgia, even though I still live close to the Alps.

References

Abruzzo, Margaret. 2011. *Polemical Pain: Slavery, Cruelty, and the Rise of Humanitarianism*. Baltimore: The Johns Hopkins University Press.

Agence France-Press. 2021. 'La leyenda de los "French Doctors" en un Afganistán bajo la ocupación soviética'. *Swissinfo*. www.swissinfo.ch/spa/la-leyenda-de-los–french-doctors–en-un-afganistán-bajo-la-ocupación-soviética/46683816.

Alaimo, Stacey. 2019. 'Introduction: Science Studies and the Blue Humanities'. *Configurations* 27 (4): 429–32.

Arendt, Hannah. 1958. *The Human Condition*. Chicago: University of Chicago Press.

Arendt, Hannah. 2006a. *On Revolution*. London: Penguin Books.

Arendt, Hannah. 2006b. *Eichmann in Jerusalem: A Report on the Banality of Evil*. London: Penguin.

Arrizabalaga, Jon and Àlvar Martínez-Vidal. 2022. 'Medicine, Religion, and the Humanitarian Ethos: Walter B. Cannon, Unitarianism, and the Care of Spanish Republican Refugees in France'. *Journal of the History of Medicine and Allied Sciences* 77 (2): 158–85.

Barclay, Katie. 2021. 'State of the Field: The History of Emotions'. *History* 106 (371): 456–66.

Barnes, Diana and Delia Falconer. 2020. 'Compassion, a Timely Feeling . . . '. *Emotions: History, Culture, Society* 4 (1): 91–108.

Barnett, Michael. 2011. *Empire of Humanity: A History of Humanitarianism*. Ithaca: Cornell University Press.

Barnett, Michael. 2014. 'Refugees and Humanitarianism'. In *The Oxford Handbook of Refugee and Forced Migration*, edited by Elena Fiddian-Qasmiyeh and Gil Loescher, 242–53. Oxford: Oxford University Press.

Bertschinger, Claire. 1980–1990. *What They Don't Teach You in Geneva, Security Guidelines on the Field*. Claire Bertschinger's private collection.

Boddice, Rob. 2016. *The Science of Sympathy: Morality, Evolution, and Victorian Civilization*. Urbana: University of Illinois Press.

Boddice, Rob. 2018. 'The History of Emotions: Past, Present, Future'. *Revista de Estudios Sociales* 62: 10–15.

Boddice, Rob. 2019. *A History of Feelings*. London: Reaktion Books.

Boddice, Rob. 2021. *Humane Professions: The Defence of Experimental Medicine, 1876–1914*. Cambridge: Cambridge University Press.

Boddice, Rob. 2022. 'Authenticity and the Dynamics of Experience'. *Digital Handbook of the History of Experience*. https://sites.tuni.fi/hexhandbook/theory/rob-boddice-again-authenticity-and-the-dynamics-of-experience/.

Boddice, Rob and Mark Smith. 2020. *Emotion, Sense and Experience*. Cambridge: Cambridge University Press.

Bourke, Joanna. 2005. *Fear: A Cultural History*. London: Virago.

Bourke, Joanna. 2015. *What It Means to Be Human: Reflections from 1791 to the Present*. London: Virago.

Braudel, Fernand. 1999. *La Méditerranée: L'espace et l'histoire*. Paris: Flammarion.

Brauman, Rony. 2000. 'L'humanitaire par-delà la légende'. *Études* 5 (392): 615–26.

Brauman, Rony. 2012. 'Médecins Sans Frontières and the ICRC: Matters of Principle'. *International Review of the Red Cross* 98 (888): 1523–35.

Brudholm, Thomas. 2008. *Resentment's Virtue: Jean Amery and the Refusal to Forgive*. Philadelphia: Temple University.

Burton, Antoinette. 1994. *Burdens of History: British Feminist, Indian Women, and Imperial Culture, 1865–1915*. Chapel Hill: The University of North Carolina Press.

Butler, Judith. 1990. *Gender Trouble: Feminism and the Subversion of Identity*. New York: Routledge.

Byrne, Justin. 2007. 'From Brookline to Belchite: New Yorkers in the Abraham Lincoln Brigade'. In *Facing Fascism: New York and the Spanish Civil War*, edited by Peter N. Carroll and James D. Fernández, 72–82. New York: New York University Press.

Cassel, Avery, Diane Kanzler, Diego Gomez and Laura Antoniou. 2018. *Resistance: The LGTB Fight Against Fascism in WWII*. Dana Point: Stacked Deck Press.

Chenery, Thomas. 1854. 'The Crimea'. *The Times*, 12 October: 6–7.

Cohn, Carol. 2012. *Women and Wars: Contested Histories, Uncertain Futures*. Malden, MA: Polity.

Cotter, Cedric. 2016. (S') *Aider pour survivre: action humanitaire et neutralité suisse pendant la Première Guerre mondiale*. Thèse de doctorat. Université de Genève.

Crombrugghe, Ida. 1871. *Journal d'une infirmière pendant la guerre de 1870–71: Sarrebruck, Metz, Cambrai*. Bruxelles: Librairie polyglotte de F. Classen.

Darrow, Margaret H. 1996. 'French Volunteer Nursing and the Myth of War Experience in World War I'. *The American Historical Review* 101 (1): 80–106.

Daston, Lorraine. 1995. 'The Moral Economy of Science'. *Osiris* 10: 2–24.

Davy, Eleanor. 2015. *Idealism beyond Borders: The French Revolutionary Left and the Rise of Humanitarianism, 1954–1988.* Cambridge: Cambridge University Press.

Dejung, Christof. 2011. 'Beyond the Alpine Myth, across the Linguistic Ditch: Cultural History in Switzerland'. In *Cultural History in Europe: Institutions - Themes-Perspectives*, edited by Jörg Rogge, 157–70. Bielefeld: Transcript Verlag.

de la Bellacasa, María P. 2017. *Matters of Care: Speculative Ethics in More than Human Worlds.* Minneapolis: University of Minnesota Press.

Desgrandchamps, Marie-Luce. 2011. 'Revenir sur le mythe fondateur de Médecins sans frontières: les relations entre les médecins français et le CICR pendant la guerre du Biafra (1967–1970)'. *Relations internationales* 146: 95–108.

Desgrandchamps, Marie-Luce. 2018. *L'humanitaire en guerre civile: la crise du Biafra (1967–1970).* Rennes: Presses universitaires de Rennes.

Dixon, Thomas. 2020. 'What is the History of Anger a History of?' *Emotions: History, Culture, Society* 4 (1): 1–34.

Dobbie, Imogen. 2020. 'Making the Maritime Visible: Rethinking Humanitarianism at Sea'. *Rethinking Refugee Platform.* www.rsc.ox.ac.uk/news/rethinking-humanitarianism-at-sea-imogen-dobie.

Dodman, Thomas. 2018. *What Nostalgia Was: War, Empire, and the Time of Deadly Emotion.* Chicago: Chicago University Press.

Donlon, Anne. 2019. 'Thyra Edwards's Spanish War Scrapbook'. In *To Turn the Whole World Over: Black Women and Internationalism*, edited by Keisha N. Blain and Tiffany M. Gill, 101–22. Urbana: University of Illinois Press.

Drenth, van Annemiecke and Francisca de Haan. 1999. *The Rise of Caring Power: Elizabeth Fry and Josephine Butler in Britain and the Netherlands.* Amsterdam: Amsterdam University Press.

Leuthy, Johann Jakob. 1848. *Récit des derniers événements survenus en Suisse, par suite de l'appel des jésuites à Lucerne et de l'alliance séparée (Sonderbund).* Berne: Henri Fischer éditeurs.

Dunant, Henry. 1947. *A Memory of Solferino.* Geneva: ICRC. First published in 1862.

Eckstein, Guy. 2017. *Discours lors de la présentation du film La lumière de l'espoir.* Geneva: Cinémas du Grütli.

Edgar, Brenda L. 2022. 'Archiving Trauma of Internment Camps in Film: Jacqueline Veuve's Journal de Rivesaltes, 1941–1942 (1997)'. In *Making Humanitarian Crises: Emotions and Images in History*, edited by Brenda L. Edgar, Valérie Gorin and Dolores Martín-Moruno, 101–26. Cham: Palgrave Macmillan.

Eidenbenz, Elisabeth. 1938a. *Letter to Her Family from Burjassot*. 6 February. NL 4 Eidenbenz. 1. Biografisches Material. 4. Archiv für Zeitgeschichte (Zürich).

Eidenbenz, Elisabeth. 1938b. *Letter to Her Family from Madrid*. 7 March. NL 4 Eidenbenz. Archiv für Zeitgeschichte (Zürich).

Eidenbenz, Elisabeth. 1938c. *Letter to Her Family from Burjassot*. 6 February. NL 4 Eidenbenz. 1. Biografisches Material. Archiv für Zeitgeschichte (Zürich).

Eidenbenz, Elisabeth. 2008. *Letter from Elisabeth Eidenbenz to Guy Eckstein*. 7 April. Eckstein Private Archives.

Enloe, Cynthia. 1989. *Bananas: Beaches and Bases: Making Feminist Sense of International Politics*. Berkeley: University of California Press.

Everly, Katryn. 2022a. 'Intersectional Silencing in the Archive: Salaria Kea and the Spanish Civil War'. *Languages, Literatures, and Linguistics* 3 (30): 1–17.

Everly, Katryn. 2022b. 'Salaria Kea in the Archive'. *The Volunteer* 40 (1): 10–11.

Eyice, Mari. 2021. 'When Feelings Grow Cold: What to Do Next in the History of Emotions'. *Lychnos*: 295–310.

Fassin, Didier. 2009. 'Moral Economies Revisited'. *Annales: Histoire, Sciences Sociales* 64 (6): 1237–66.

Fassin, Didier. 2012. *Humanitarian Reason: A Moral History of the Present*. Berkeley: University of California Press.

Favez, Jean-Claude. 1988. *Une mission impossible? Le CICR, les déportations et les camps de concentration nazis*. Lausanne: Payot.

Febvre, Lucien. 1973. 'Sensibility and History: How to Reconstitute the Emotional Life of the Past?' In *A New Kind of History: From the Writings of Febvre*, edited by Peter Burke and translated by Keith Folca, 12–26. London: Routledge.

Fischer-Tiné, Harald. 2015. 'The Other Side of Internationalism: Switzerland as a Hub of Militant Anti-Colonialism'. In *Colonial Switzerland: Rethinking Colonialism from the Margins*, 221–58. Houndsmills: Palgrave Macmillan.

Fournot, Juliette. 2006. *À Ciel Ouverte*. Edition Dupuis/Aire Libre. Kanari Films.

Fournot, Juliette. 2022. 'Mission clandestine en Afghanistan'. *MSF*. www.msf.fr/actualites/podcast-mission-clandestine-en-afghanistan.

Frevert, Ute. 2011. *Emotions in History: Lost and Found*. Budapest: Central European University Press.

Frevert, Ute. 2014. *The Moral Economy of Trust: Modern Trajectories*. The 2013 Annual Lecture. London: German Historical Institute.

Frevert, Ute. 2016. 'The History of Emotions'. In *Handbook of Emotions, Fourth Edition*, edited by Lisa F. Barret, Michael Lewis and Jeannette M. Haviland-Jones, 49–65. New York: The Guildford Press.

Frevert, Ute. 2019. *Moral Economies*. Göttingen: Vadenhoeck & Ruprecht.

Frevert, Ute. 2020. *The Politics of Humiliation: A Modern History*. Oxford: Oxford University Press.

Galeano, Eduardo. 1993. *Las Palabras Andantes*. Montevideo: Ediciones del Chanchito.

Galeano, Eduardo. 2001. *Upside Down: A Primer for the Looking-Glass World*. New York: Picador.

Gatrell, Peter. 2014. 'Refugees'. *International Encyclopedia of the First World War*. https://encyclopedia.1914-1918-online.net/article/refugees.

Gill, Rebecca. 2013. *Calculating Compassion: Humanity and relief in war, Britain 1870–1914*. Manchester: Manchester University Press.

Gorin, Valérie. 2013. 'La couverture médiatique de la guerre civile du Biafra au regard des enjeux humanitaires dans les médias français, suisses et américains (1967–1970)'. *Le Temps de Médias* 2 (21): 176–95.

Green, Abigail. 2014. 'Humanitarianism in Nineteenth-Century Context: Religious, Gendered, National'. *The Historical Journal* 57 (4): 1157–75.

Green, Blake. 1977. 'The Angels of the Last "Pure War"'. *San Francisco Chronicle*, 10 February: 22. (Preserved at Fredericka Martin Papers, ALBA 00, Series I, Box 6, Folder 23, Tamiment Library, New York University).

Gregory, James. 2022. *Mercy and British Culture, 1760–1960*. London: Bloomsbury.

Grellety-Bosviel, Pascal. 2013. *Toute une vie d'humanitaire, 50 ans de terrain d'un médecin-carnettiste*. Bordeaux: Elytis.

Guibert, Emmanuel, Didier Lefèvre and Frédéric Lemercier. 2008. *The Photographer: Into War-torn Afghanistan with Doctors without Borders*. New York: First Second Books.

Halttunen, Karen. 1995. 'Humanitarianism and the Pornography of Pain'. *The American Historical Review* 100 (2): 303–34.

Hass, Peter M. 1992. 'Epistemic Communities and International Policy Coordination'. *International Organization* 46 (1): 1–35.

Hoegaerts, Josephine and Stephanie Olsen. 2021. 'The History of Experience: Afterword'. In *Lived Nation as the History of Experiences and Emotions in Finland, 1800–2000*, edited by Ville Kivimäki, Sami Suodenjoki and Tanja Vahtikari, 375–83. Cham: Palgrave Macmillan.

Huber, Anja. 2018. 'Exile and Migration'. *International Encyclopedia of the First World War*. https://encyclopedia.1914-1918-online.net/article/exile_and_migration_switzerland.

Hughes, Langston. 1964. *I Wonder as I Wander: An Autobiographical Journey.* New York: Hill and Wang.

Hughes, Langston. 1994. *The Collected Poems of Langston Hughes*, edited by Arnold Rampersad and David Roessel. New York: Vintage Books.

Humbert, Laure, Marie-Luce Desgrandchamps, Bertrand Taithe and Raphaële Balu. 2021. 'New Approaches to Medical Care, Humanitarianism and Violence during the "Long" Second World War, c. 1931–1953'. Seminar Series Organised by the AHRC Project. *Colonial and Transnational Intimacies: Medical Humanitarianism in the French External Resistance.* https://colonialandtransnationalintimacies.com/seminar-series/.

Hutchinson, John F. 1996. *Champions of Charity: War and the Rise of the Red Cross.* Colorado: Westview Press.

Ibbett, Katherine. 2018. *Compassion's Edge: Fellow-Feeling and Its Limits in Early Modern France.* Philadelphia: University of Pennsylvania Press.

Im Hof-Piguet, Anne-Marie. 1985. *La Filière en France occupée 1942-1944.* Yverdon-les-Bains: Éditions de la Thièle.

Ingersoll, Karin A. 2016. *Waves of Knowing: A Seascape Epistemology.* Durham: Duke University Press.

Jay, Martin. 2005. *Songs of Experience: Modern American and European Variations on a Universal Theme.* Berkley: University of California Press.

Katajala-Peltomaa and Maria Toivo. 2022. 'Three Levels of Experience'. *Digital Handbook of the History of Experience.* https://sites.tuni.fi/hexhandbook/theory/three-levels-of-experience/.

Kea, Salaria. Undated a. *While Passing through.* Frances Patai Papers, ALBA 131, Box 2, Folder 12.

Kea, Salaria. Undated b. *May Every Knock Be a Boost.* Frances Patai Papers, ALBA 131, Box 2, Folder 12.

Kea, Salaria. Undated c. *Memoir (Typescript).* Fredericka Martin Papers, ALBA 001, Series 1, Box 9, Folder 33. Tamiment Library/Robert F. Wagner Labor Archives, New York University.

Kea, Salaria. 1938. *A Negro Nurse in Republican Spain.* New York: The Negro Committee to Aid Spain with the Medical Bureau and North American Committee to Aid Spanish Democracy.

Kea, Salaria. 1980. Salaria Kea O'Reilly Interview John Gerassi Oral History Collection; ALBA.AUDIO.018; Box number 1; Folder numbers 18-152 to 18-153. Tamiment Library, Robert F. Wagner Labor Archives, New York University.

Kivimäki, Ville, Sami Suodenjoki and Tanja Vahtikari. 2021. *Lived Nation as the History of Experiences and Emotions in Finland, 1800–2000.* Cham: Palgrave Macmillan.

Klemp, Pia. 2022. *Wutschrift: Wände enreissen, ansttat sie hochzugehen.* München: Penguin Verlag.

Klemp, Pia. 2019. 'Why I Fight for Solidarity'. *TEDxBerlin.* www.youtube.com/ watch?v=-7V1zNNfc_Q.

Klemp, Pia. 2021. *Les vivants, les morts et les marins.* Paris: Fleuve Éditions.

Klemp, Pia. 2022. Wutschrift: Wände einreissen, anstatt sie hochzugehen. München: Penguin Verlag.

Klimke, Martin, Reinhild Kreis and Christian F. Ostermann (eds.). 2016. 'Introduction'. In *Trust, But Verify: The Politics of Uncertainty and the Transformation of the Cold War Order, 1969–1991*, 1–14. Chicago: Stanford University Press.

Konstan, David. 2001. *Pity Transformed.* London: Duckworth.

Laqueur, Thomas W. 1989. 'Bodies, Details, and the Humanitarian Narrative'. In *The New Cultural History*, edited by Lynn Hunt, 176–204. Berkley: University of California Press.

Leese, Peter. 2022. 'The Limits of Trauma: Experience and Narrative in Europe c.1945'. In *Trauma, Experience and Narrative in Europe after World War II*, edited by Ville Kivimäki and Peter Leese, 3–26. Cham: Palgrave Macmillan.

Leyder, Marie. 2020. 'The American and Canadian wartime godmothers of Belgian soldiers: Joseph de Dorlodot's Correspondence and Documentation Office (1915–1919)'. *Medicine, Conflict and Survival* 36 (1): 82–102.

Louis-Courvoiser, Micheline. 2019. 'Inquiétude/Uneasinnes: Between Mental Emotion and Bodily Sensation (18th–20th centuries)'. *Emotions: History, Culture, Society* 3: 94–115.

Maier, Marietta and Daniela Saxer (eds.). 2007. 'Die Pragmatik der Emotionen im 19. und 20. Jahrhundert'. *Traverse* 2: 7–10.

Martín-Moruno, Dolores. 2016a. 'Pain as Practice in Paolo Mantegazza's Science of Emotions'. *Osiris* 31 (1): 137–62.

Martín-Moruno, Dolores. 2016b. 'Salaria Kea's Memories from the Spanish Civil War'. Paper Presented at the Conference. *Warriors without Weapons: Humanitarian Action during the Spanish Civil War and the Republican Exile.* The Louis Jeantet Foundation, Geneva, 27th October.

Martín-Moruno, Dolores. 2019. 'Fearful Female Bodies: The Pétroleuses of the Paris Commune'. In *Emotional Bodies: The Historical Performativity of Emotions*, edited by Dolores Martín-Moruno and Beatriz Pichel, 175–94. Urbana: University of Illinois Press.

Martín-Moruno, Dolores. 2020a. 'Faut-il brûler l'histoire des émotions'. *Traverse* 2: 147–56.

Martín-Moruno, Dolores. 2020b. 'Introduction: Feeling humanitarianism during the Spanish Civil War and Republican Exile'. *Journal of Spanish Cultural Studies* 21 (4): 445–57.

Martín-Moruno, Dolores. 2020c. 'Elisabeth Eidenbenz's Humanitarian Experience during Spanish Civil War and the Republican Exile'. *Journal of Spanish Cultural Studies* 21 (4): 485–502.

Martín-Moruno, Dolores. 2022. 'Crisis? What Crisis? Making Humanitarian Crises Visible in the History of Emotions'. In *Making Humanitarian Crises: Emotions and Images in History*, edited by Brenda L. Edgar, Valérie Gorin and Dolores Martín-Moruno, 1–28. Cham: Palgrave Macmillan.

Martín-Moruno, Dolores. 2023a. 'Physiologies of Love'. In *A Cultural History of Love in the Modern Age*, Vol. 6, edited by Claire Langhammer. London: Bloomsbury. (In press).

Martín-Moruno, Dolores. 2023b. 'Pain(ful) Experiences as an Archipelago of Knowledge(s)'. *Digital Handbook of the History of Experiences*. https://sites.tuni.fi/hexhandbook/theory/painful-experiences-as-an-archipelago-of-knowledges/.

Martín-Moruno, Dolores and Beatriz Pichel. 2019. *Emotional Bodies: The Historical Performativity of Emotions*. Urbana: University of Illinois Press.

Martín-Moruno, Dolores, Brenda L. Edgar and Marie Leyder. 2020. 'Feminist Perspectives on the History of Humanitarian Relief'. *Medicine, Conflict and Survival* 36 (1): 2–18.

Martinez, Julie. 2013. 'Le retrouvailles en Périge or des héros du "Photographe"'. *Sud-Ouest*. www.sudouest.fr/dordogne/bassillac/les-retrouvailles-en-perig-ord-des-heros-du-photographe-8586085.php.

Möller, Esther, Johannes Paulmann and Katharina Storning. 2020. *Gendering Global Humanitarianism in the Twentieth Century: Practice, Politics and the Power of Representation*. Cham: Palgrave.

Monsutti, Alessandro. 2005. *War and Migration: Social Networks and Economic Strategies of the Hazaras of Afghanistan*. New York: Routledge.

Moscoso, Javier. 2012. *Pain: A Cultural History*. Houndmills: Palgrave Macmillan.

Nagy, Piroska, Véronique Frandon, David El Kenz, Matthias Grässlin. 1994. 'Pour une histoire de la souffrance: Expressions, représentations, usages'. *Médiévales* 27: 5–14.

Nagy, Piroska and Xavier Biron-Ouellet. 2020. 'A Collective Emotion in Medieval Italy: The Flagellant Movement of 1260'. *Emotion Review* 12 (3): 135–45.

Nagy, Piroska and Xavier Biron-Ouellet. 2022. 'Pour une histoire de l'expérience: le laboratoire médiéval'. *Memini* 28. https://journals.openedi tion.org/memini/2192#quotation

Newman, Julia. 2002. *American Women during the Spanish Civil War*. New York: Exemplary Films.

Ngai, Sianne. 2005. *Ugly Feelings*. Cambridge, MA: Harvard University Press.

Nightingale, Florence. 1860. *Notes on Nursing: What It Is, and What It Is Not*. New York: D. Appleton.

Nightingale, Florence. 1864. *Two Letters to Thomas Longmore*. Wellcome RACM/1139 LP54/7-8.

Nightingale, Florence. 1872. *Lettre de Mme Florence Nightingale à M. Henry Dunant*. ICRC Archives. V-P-HIST_E-01620.

Nightingale, Florence. 1997. *Letters from the Crimea*, edited by Sue M. Goldie. Manchester: Mandolin.

Oppermann, Serpil. 2019. 'Storied Seas and Living Metaphors in Blue Humanities'. *Configurations* 27 (4): 443–61.

Patai, Frances. 1990. *Letter to Martin Balter*. 7 December. Frances Patai Papers. Tamiment Library, Robert F. Wagner Labor Archives, TS. Frances Patai papers.

Patai, Frances. 1995. 'Heroine of the Good Fight: Testimonies of U.S Volunteer Nurses in the Spanish Civil War, 1936–1939'. *Nursing History Review* 3: 79–104.

Pearson, Emma M., and Louisa E. McLaughlin. 1871. *Our Adventures during the War of 1870*. London: Richard Bentley.

Pedwell, Carolyn. 2014. *Affective Relations: The Transnational Politics of Empathy*. Houndmills: Palgrave Macmillan.

Perigüell, Emilio B., and Rosa B. Añón. 2003. *Real expedición filantrópica de la vacuna: 1803–1806*. Madrid: Ministerio de Sanidad y Consumo.

Philips, Carla R. 2020. 'Why Did Anyone Got to Sea? Structures of Maritime Enlistment for Family Tradition to Violent Coercion'. In *A World at Sea: Maritime Practices and Global History*, edited by Lauren Benton and Nathan Perl-Rosenthal, 17–36. Philadelphia: University of Pennsylvania Press.

Plamper, Ian. 2015. *The History of Emotions: An Introduction*. Oxford: Oxford University Press.

Prieto, Moisés. 2018. 'El estudio de las emociones en Latinoamérica'. *Iberoamericana: América Latina, España, Portugal* 18 (67): 223–46.

Prieto, Moisés. 2020. 'Erasing the Fear from the Eyes: A Micro-Narrative on Emotions in Spanish Migration to Cold-War Switzerland'. *Emotions, Culture and Society* 4 (2): 252–78.

Prieto, Moisés. 2021. '"Dieser is auch für's Vaterland gestorben": Tod und Gedenken in den Nachwehen des Schweizerischen Sonderbundkrieges (1847)'. In *Tod und Krise: Totenfürsorge und Besttungspraktiken im langen 19: Jahrhundert*, edited by Anja Maria Hamann, Nina Kreibig and Katja Martin, 112–40. Postdam: Arijeh.

Purtschert, Patricia and Harald-Fischer Tiné (eds.). 2015. *Colonial Switzerland: Rethinking Colonialism from the Margins*. Houndsmills: Palgrave Macmillan.

Quesada, Carmen C. 2019. 'Salaria Kea and the Spanish Civil War'. In *Black USA and Spain: Shared Memories in the 20th Century*, edited by Rosalía Cornejo-Parriego, 113–33. New York: Routledge.

Ramusack, Barbara. 1992. 'Cultural Missionaries, Maternal Imperialist, Feminist Allies: British Women Activist in India, 1865–1945'. In *Western Women and Imperialism: Complicity and Resistance*, edited by Nupur Chaudhuri and Margaret Strobel, 119–36. Bloomington: Indiana University Press.

Reddy, William. 2001. *The Navigation of Feeling: A Framework for the History of Emotions*. New York: Cambridge University Press.

Revel, Jacques. 1996. *Jeux d'échelles: La micro-analyse à l'expérience*. Paris: Gallimard-Le Seuil.

Rodogno, Davide. 2020. 'Certainty, Compassion and the Ingrained Arrogance of Humanitarians'. In *The Red Cross Movement: Myths, Practices and Turning Points*, edited by James Crossland, Melanie Oppenheim and Neville Wylie, 27–44. Manchester: Manchester University Press.

Roger, Noëlle. 1915a. *Les carnets d'une infirmière*. Paris: Attinger Frères.

Roger, Noëlle. 1915b. *Le carnet d'un témoin: Le train de grands blessés*. Paris: Attinger Frères.

Roger, Noëlle. 1991. Noëlle Roger's Papers. CH BGE Ms. Fr. 6161-6272.

Rosenwein, Barbara. 2002. 'Worrying about Emotions in History'. *The American Historical Review* 107 (3): 821–45.

Rosenwein, Barbara. 2006. *Emotional Communities in the Early Middle Ages*. Ithaca: Cornell University Press.

Rosenwein, Barbara H. 2020. *Anger: The Conflicted History of an Emotion*. New Haven and London: Yale University Press.

Rufin, Jean-Christophe. 1986. *Le piège: Quand l'aide humanitaire remplace la guerre*. Paris: J.-C Lattès.

Salvatici, Silvia. 2019. *A History of Humanitarianism, 1755–1989: In the Name of Others*. Manchester: Manchester University Press.

Sartre, Jean-Paul. 1968. 'Genocide'. *New Left Review* 1 (48): 13–25.

Scaglia, Ilaria. 2020a. *The Emotions of Internationalism: Feeling International Cooperation in the Alps in the Interwar Period*. Oxford: Oxford University Press.

Scaglia, Ilaria. 2020b. 'The Politics of Internationalism Rest on the Intimacy of Feelings'. *Psyche Aeon*. https://psyche.co/ideas/the-politics-of-international ism-rest-on-the-intimacy-of-feelings.

Scheer, Monique. 2012. 'Are Emotions a Kind of Practice (and Is That What Makes Them Have a History)?: A Bourdieuian Approach to Understanding Emotion'. *History and Theory* 51: 193–220.

Scott, Joan W. 1991. 'The Evidence of Experience'. *Critical Inquiry* 17 (4): 773–97.

Seacole, Mary. 2005. *Wonderful Adventures of Mrs Seacole in Many Lands*. London: Penguin.

Sharpe, Emily R. 2011. 'Salaria Kea's Spanish memoirs'. *The Volunteer*. https:// albavolunteer.org/2011/12/salaria-keas-spanish-memoirs/.

Sharpe, Emily R. 2020. *Mosaic Fictions: Writing Identity in the Spanish Civil War*. Toronto: University of Toronto Press.

Slim, Hugo. 2020. 'You Don't Have to Be Neutral to Be a Good Humanitarian'. *The New Humanitarian*. www.thenewhumanitarian.org/opinion/2020/08/27/ humanitarian-principles-neutrality.

Smith, Adam. 1767. *The Theory of Moral Sentiments*. London: A. Millar, A Kincaid and J. Bell.

Solera, Gianluca. 2017. *Citizen Activism and Mediterranean Identity: Beyond Eurocentrism*. Cham: Palgrave Macmillan.

Starobinski, Jean. 1966. 'The Idea of Nostalgia'. *Diogenes* 14 (54): 81–103.

Starobinski, Jean. 1993. *Blessing in Disguise; or, The Morality of Evil*. Cambridge, MA: Harvard University Press.

Stoler, Ann L. 2004. 'Affective States'. In *A Companion to the Anthropology of Politics*, edited by David Nugent and Joan Vincent, 4–20. New York: Wiley.

Taithe, Bertrand. 2001. *Citizenship and Wars: France in Turmoil 1870–1871*. London: Routledge.

Taithe, Bertrand. 2006. '"Cold Calculation in the Faces of Horrors?" Pity, Compassion and the Making of Humanitarian Protocols'. In *Medicine, Emotion and Disease, 1700–1950*, edited by Fay B. Alberti, 79–99. Houndmills: Palgrave Macmillan.

Taithe, Bertrand. 2016. 'The Cradle of the New Humanitarian System? International Work and European Volunteers at the Cambodian Border Camps, 1979–1993'. *Contemporary European History* 25 (2): 335–58.

Taithe, Bertrand. 2019. 'Demotic Humanitarians: Historical Perspectives on the Global Reach of Local Initiatives, 1940–2017'. *Third World Quarterly* 40 (10): 1781–98.

Taithe, Bertrand. 2020. 'Humanitarian Masculinity: Desire, Character and Heroics'. In *Gendering Global Humanitarianism in the Twentieth Century: Practice, Politics and the Power of Representation*, edited by Esther Möller, Johannes Paulmann and Katharina Storning, 1–32. Netherlands: Palgrave Macmillan.

Taithe, Bertrand and John Borton. 2015. 'History, Memory and "Lessons Learnt" for Humanitarian Practitioners'. *European Review of History* 23 (1–2): 210–24.

Thompson, Edward P. 1971. 'The Moral Economy of the English Crowd in the Eighteenth Century'. *Past & Present* 50: 76–136.

Fisher, Berenice and Joan C. Tronto. 1990. 'Towards a Feminist Theory of Caring'. In *Circles of Care: Work and Identity in Women's Lives*, edited by Emily K. Abel and Margaret K. Nelson, 36–54. Albany: SUNY Press.

Valas, Patrick-Jean-René. 1969. *Organisation et résultats du travail d'une équipe médico-chirurgicale de la Croix-Rouge au Biafra*. Thèse. Faculté de Médecine de Paris.

Veuve, Jacqueline. 1987. *La Filière*. Geneva: ACHIPROD.

Veuve, Jacqueline. 1991. *Les émotions helvétiques*. Cinémathèque Suisse, Film et Video Productions. Limbo Film AG, TSR.

Veuve, Jacqueline. 1997. *Journal de Rivesaltes 1941–42*. Ciné Manufacture CMS, SA, RTS Radio Télévision Suisse.

Vidal, Fernando. 2020. 'The History of Medicine and the Reasons of the Body'. *Mefisto*: *Rivista di medicina, filosofia e storia* 4 (2): 63–88.

Weber, Olivier. 1995. *French doctors: l'épopée des hommes et des femmes qui ont inventé la médecine humanitaire*. Paris: Robert Lafont.

Zucconi, Francesco. 2018. *Displacing Caravaggio: Art, Media, and Humanitarian Visual Culture*. Cham: Palgrave Macmillan.

Acknowledgements

This Element would not have been possible without the support of the Swiss National Science Foundation (hereafter SNSF), which has granted me with several projects during the last six years: the SNSF Professorship project 'Those women who performed humanitarian action: A Gendered history of compassion from the Franco-Prussian War to the Second World War', its first-year extension 'Lived Humanitarianism: Gender, Experiences and Knowledge(s)', its second-year extension 'A Polyphonic History of Care: Gender, Experiences and Humanitarian Knowledge(s)' and its related public outreach project 'Beyond Compassion: Gender and Humanitarian Action.' Fortunately, this Element is not just the result of the research which I have conducted alone; I must express my gratitude to Camille Bajeux, Brenda Lynn Edgar, Marie Leyder and Gian Marco Vidor for having made my project their own when they became the members of the team which I have led at the University of Geneva since 2017.

Special thanks also must be extended to the collaborators who have integrated the network that has resulted from these projects: Jon Arrizabalaga (CSIC, Spain), Roland Bleiker and Emma Hutchinson (University of Queensland), Rob Boddice and Stephanie Olsen (Tampere University), Rony Brauman (CRASH, Paris), Delphine Gardey (Institute of Gender Studies, University of Geneva), Rebecca Gill (University of Huddersfield), Valérie Gorin (Geneva Centre of Humanitarian Studies), Pascal Hufschmid (International Red Cross and Red Crescent Museum), Laure Humbert and Bertrand Taithe (University of Manchester), Jo Labanyi (New York University), Patrizia Lombardo (Faculty of Letters, University of Geneva), Àlvar Martínez-Vidal (Universitat de València), Beatriz Pichel (De Monfort University, Leicester) and Davide Rodogno (Geneva Graduate Institute). I am indebted to Guy Eckstein and Juliette Fournot who shared their testimonies with me, as well as to the members of the Centre of Excellence in the History of Experiences (Tampere University) and the Centre for the History of Emotions (Max-Planck Institute) with whom I discussed some of the ideas presented here. I would also like to thank Elne's city hall, which kindly provided me with permission to reproduce Elisabeth Eidenbenz's photograph in this Element. I would like to dedicate this Element to Hannah, Léonide, André and François as they have taught me how to live my Swissness with plenitude, despite the fact that the heights of the mountains in the Alps still provoke feelings of vertigo within me.

**Swiss National
Science Foundation**

Author Biography

Dolores Martín-Moruno is Swiss National Science Foundation Professor at the Institute for Ethics, History and the Humanities at the Faculty of Medicine of the University of Geneva, Switzerland. She has published widely on the history of emotions and the history of humanitarian relief. She is the author/editor of five books, including *Emotional Bodies: The Historical Performativity of Emotions* with Beatriz Pichel (University of Illinois Press, 2019) and *Making Humanitarian Crises: Emotions and Images in History* with Brenda Lynn Edgar and Valérie Gorin (Palgrave Macmillan, 2022).

Cambridge Elements ≡

Histories of Emotions and the Senses

Series Editors

Rob Boddice
Tampere University

Rob Boddice (PhD, FRHistS) is Senior Research Fellow at the Academy of Finland Centre of Excellence in the History of Experiences. He is the author/editor of 13 books, including *Knowing Pain: A History of Sensation, Emotion and Experience* (Polity Press, 2023), *Humane Professions: The Defence of Experimental Medicine, 1876–1914* (Cambridge University Press, 2021) and *A History of Feelings* (Reaktion, 2019).

Piroska Nagy
Université du Québec à Montréal (UQAM)

Piroska Nagy is Professor of Medieval History at the Université du Québec à Montréal (UQAM) and initiated the first research program in French on the history of emotions. She is the author or editor of 14 volumes, including *Le Don des larmes au Moyen Âge* (Albin Michel, 2000); *Medieval Sensibilities: A History of Emotions in the Middle Ages*, with Damien Boquet (Polity, 2018); and *Histoire des émotions collectives: Épistémologie, émergences, expériences*, with D. Boquet and L. Zanetti Domingues (Classiques Garnier, 2022).

Mark Smith
University of South Carolina

Mark Smith (PhD, FRHistS) is Carolina Distinguished Professor of History and Director of the Institute for Southern Studies at the University of South Carolina. He is author or editor of over a dozen books and his work has been translated into Chinese, Korean, Danish, German, and Spanish. He has lectured in Europe, throughout the United States, Australia, and China and his work has been featured in *The New York Times*, the *London Times*, *The Washington Post*, and *The Wall Street Journal*. He serves on the US Commission for Civil Rights.

About the Series

Born of the emotional and sensory 'turns', *Elements in Histories of Emotions and the Senses* move one of the fastest-growing interdisciplinary fields forward. The series is aimed at scholars across the humanities, social sciences, and life sciences, embracing insights from a diverse range of disciplines, from neuroscience to art history and economics. Chronologically and regionally broad, encompassing global, transnational, and deep history, it concerns such topics as affect theory, intersensoriality, embodiment, human-animal relations, and distributed cognition. The founding editor of the series was Jan Plamper.

Cambridge Elements $\equiv$

Histories of Emotions and the Senses

A full series listing is available at: www.cambridge.org/EHES

Printed in the United States
by Baker & Taylor Publisher Services